TESTIMONIES

OF

GOD'S LOVE

BOOK 5

Cover Design by Del Hall IV
Cover Image by TTstudio/shutterstock.com

ISBN: 978-1-947255-00-5

TESTIMONIES

OF

GOD'S LOVE

BOOK 5

Del Hall and Del Hall IV

Acknowledgments

It is with the deepest love and gratitude we thank all those who contributed to this book. The willingness to share some of their sacred experiences made this book possible. These testimonies show so much more is possible in your relationship with God. We hope reading them will inspire you to more fully accept the Hand of God.

The authors would also like to thank all those who helped in the editing of this book: Joan Clickner, Lorraine Fortier, and Terry Kisner. Your keen eyes and thoughtful suggestions made a huge difference in the telling of these profound stories.

"The days of any religion or path coming between me and my children are coming to an end" saith the Lord

December 29, 2013

Table of Contents

Foreword xiii

Introduction 1

Note to the Reader 5

1. Peace in My Heart 7

2. God's Guidance Leads to Abundance 11

3. I Held Her in Heaven 15

4. Something's Not Right, Do Not Leave.......... 19

5. Mom's Loveseat 22

6. I Took a Step and God Responded 26

7. Prune and Nourish 30

8. Lights On, Not Lights Out............................ 35

9. The Blue Star Before Me 39

10. Our Beloved Dog 43

11. The Love of Life.. 46

12. Prayer Answered, Not a Coincidence 51

13. A Blessed Bike Ride...................................... 57

14. More Freedom Less Worry........................... 61

15. Greater Abundance Follows

    Past-Life Healing.. 64

16. My "Unanswered" Prayer Was Answered.. 71

17. Before the Source of All 77

18. Golden Gift from God 82

19. Say What You Need to Say 89

20. Hidden Blessings... 94

21. Every Day is a Gift From God...................... 98

22. A Gift of God's Peace................................ 102

23. Confident in My Decision.......................... 105

24. A Hug Filled With God's Love................... 108

25. Reach Out and Bless Someone................. 111

26. I Finally Found Him 114

27. Gently Awoken 118

28. He Hears You — Do You Hear Him?........ 121

29. Captain's Chair 126

30. God Guided My Doctor 131

31. God's Personal Response............................137

32. Through the Eyes of Soul..........................140

33. Multiple Healings 145

34. More Love for My Cat Buster.....................159

35. God Blessed Us a Vacation 163

36. Spared by a Hair..166

37. To Do or To Be?...170

38. Reassurance in the ER 177

39. Take Me Lord! 180

40. Seeing God's Blessings..............................184

41. Soul Knows Truth 187

42. Cleansing and Preparation........................189

43. Shower in the Light 193

44. Keep My Heart Always...............................196

45. The "Little Things" in Life 199

46. Truth Uncovered 202

47. A Dream Teaching on Real Freedom........207

48. Heart of a Child...214

49. Building Divine Relationships....................217

50. The Throne of God.................................. 221

Appendix

Guidance for a Better Life "Our Story" 225

    My Father's Journey (Del Hall III).............. 225

    My Son, Del Hall IV...............................235

What is the Role of God's Prophet?............... 239

Articles of Faith ....……………………………....245

Contact Information 255

Additional Reading.. 257

Foreword

My earliest memories of childhood are of a prayer to God my three sisters and I recited every night before bedtime. I can close my eyes and still see the wooden plaque which hung above my bed. Etched into this wooden plaque were the words to a child's prayer and the figure of a little girl kneeling at the foot of her bed, with her faithful dog beside her, saying this bedtime prayer:

"Now I lay me down to sleep.
I pray the Lord my Soul to keep
If I die before I wake
I pray the Lord my Soul to take."

I was probably four years old when, for the first time, I truly listened to the words of this prayer and thought about them. I did not want to "die before I wake," but if I did, I was not afraid because I knew God loved me. I cannot tell you how I knew God loved me, I just knew He did, and I felt His loving Presence best while sitting in quiet solitude.

One of my favorite places to hide from everyone and be quiet was the hall closet where my mother and father kept their clothes. While climbing on my hands and knees and maneuvering through their shoes I discovered a small setback in the closet that was the perfect size for a small child to sit and be quiet with God. I cherished this perfect hideout and would disappear into it whenever I wished to hide from the world. I knew God loved me but was not sure sometimes of love in the world around me.

A year before attending elementary school my mother returned to work leaving me in the care of my grandmother during the day. Not understanding what was happening, I felt abandoned and uncertain of being loved. My new perfect "hideout" became our small bathroom where I could close the door and find solitude. Aware of God's Love in this solitude, I would often climb up on the bathroom counter and look closely at myself in the mirror wondering, "Who am I?" As a teenager I continued to seek God's Love in places of solitude. Now instead of the hall closet or our small bathroom, the woods became my favorite place. Finding a quiet, secluded spot, I was aware of God's Love reflected in the warmth of the sun and the singing of the birds. Time passed and these early childhood memories of God's Love faded. As an adult I still sought the peace and quiet of the woods, not recognizing I was searching for God's Love in its solitude. I did however, recognize "something" was missing in my life, but what?

My search for this "something" continued for several years. Finally with the help of friends, I was led to Guidance for a Better Life and my spiritual teacher, Del Hall III, a true Prophet of God. With Prophet's help I was blessed to discover the "something" missing in my life was recognition and acceptance of God's Love. Learning to accept the blessing and Love of God changed my life forever.

The blessings of God's Love continue, and more recently while attending a retreat Del led us in a spiritual exercise which blessed me with the beautiful gift of remembrance. It was a remembrance of my forgotten childhood prayers and memories of God's Love which I now share with you. In remembering these sacred childhood experiences of God's Love, I realized my childhood prayer to know the answer to the question "Who am I?" had also become faded and forgotten, but God did not forget! Through the process of learning the "Language of the Divine" taught lovingly by Prophet, I gradually awakened to the discovery and acceptance of who I truly am. I am Soul, an eternal Divine spark of God. My childhood prayer of long ago was remembered by God and answered. I am truly blessed.

Today, as I live my life filled with God's Love, I continue with Prophet's love and guidance to nurture a beautiful, amazing, and personal relationship with the Divine, knowing God loves me, God is always with me, and God will always be with me as I continue on my journey home to God.

It is God's Love that Soul seeks, whether our conscious mind is aware of it or not. Deep down the real eternal us, Soul, knows something is missing. The discovery of our true eternal self, Soul, goes hand in hand with finding and being able to accept the Love of God. It is my hope this book will help you, the reader, on your own journey.

Written by Donna Hospodar

Student at Guidance for a Better Life since 1995

Introduction

Welcome to book five of our "Testimonies of God's Love" series. Within these pages are fifty true stories that show the Hand of God reaching out to His children. This book, like our other books, celebrates the many varied ways God expresses His Love. God demonstrates His Love every day, but it often goes unrecognized. It is our hope that by reading these heart-warming testimonies you will learn to more fully recognize and accept God's Love in your own life. God's Love manifests in many ways from the dramatic to the very subtle. When you consciously recognize that God loves you, it can change your life. These authors have experienced this firsthand and are now building their lives on a solid foundation of knowing God personally loves them. They wish to pay it forward by helping you to do the same. Even if you recognize Divine love in your life, it is a profound blessing for God to remind you daily of His Love for you.

One of the first spiritual truths to consider, so you may more fully understand and enjoy this book, is that you do not "have" a Soul. The truth is, you ARE Soul. You are an eternal spiritual being within a temporal physical embodiment, which is to say you are Soul that has a body. In some of these stories the authors spiritually traveled into the Heavens. They traveled not in their physical bodies but as Soul. This is much like when Saint Paul shared that he knew someone who was caught up to the third Heaven. Soul can travel free of the body while still living. When the body does come to its end, the real you, SOUL, will continue on. Once again, you do not *have* a Soul; you *are* Soul that *has* a body. This seemingly simple change in perspective is actually of monumental significance. It is one of the core spiritual truths taught and experienced at Guidance for a Better Life and reflected within the testimonies of this book. When considered, or ideally experienced for yourself, it can open doors to even greater heights of wisdom, love, and understanding.

What then is Soul? In essence, Soul is an individualized piece of the Holy Spirit. We are not God, nor will we ever become God, but in a very real sense Soul is a piece of the Voice of God, the Holy Spirit. This is the true meaning behind the statement of being created in the image of God. Soul is a piece of the Holy Spirit, individualized and personalized through lifetimes of experience.

Life is busy and full of distractions making it easy to forget we are children of God, not just physical bodies. This is one reason why God always sends mankind His ordained Prophet. We need someone who sees clearly, can gently remind us that we are Soul, and who can help us soar free as spiritual eagles. God's Prophet can teach us the "Language of the Divine," the true native tongue of Soul. Then we may recognize and understand the Divine guidance that is always available for us! Fortunately, mankind is never without a Prophet. We are never alone. This is the greatest proof of God's Love for man — a continuous unbroken chain of divinely chosen and trained Prophets sent to help show us our way home to the Heart of God. As the current Prophet my father, Del Hall III, is now in this role and has been authorized to share God's Light, Love, and truth with the world.

This book is ultimately a celebration of God's Love for Soul and the many ways He expresses His Love. It is not an attempt to place a wedge between you and another spiritual teacher; it is intended to enhance whatever spiritual path you may be on, even if that is no path at all. As you may read in the Appendix, "What is the Role of God's Prophet?" you do not have to withdraw your love from a former Prophet (one who is no longer here in the physical) to benefit from being taught by the current Prophet. Having a guide who can teach you the Ways and Truths of God in both the inner spiritual worlds and also in the physical is such a blessing. Even so, if you are not comfortable accepting help from the current Prophet, there are still blessings within these pages for you. If you read this book with an open heart the testimonies within have the potential of greatly blessing you.

It is with great humility, reverence, and love that these authors share their experiences, blessings, and insights with you. They know God is truly reaching out through His Prophet to develop a more personal and loving relationship with each and every one of us. They know you too can experience even greater joy and abundance in your life by opening yourself to the truth within these pages — a truth that has the power to set you free and provide guidance for a better life.

Del Hall IV

Note to the Reader

All the authors who contributed to this book sing HU daily in spiritual contemplation. They tune in and raise up spiritually by singing HU, which makes them more receptive to the guidance and Love of God and God's Prophet. A basic understanding of both the role of God's Prophet and HU will help you more fully understand the "Language of the Divine" shared in this book. Please refer to the Appendix for an introductory understanding of God's historical line of Prophets and the role they serve.

HU is an ancient name for God that can be sung quietly or aloud in prayer. HU has existed since the beginning of time in one form or another and is available to all regardless of religion. It is a pure way to express your love to God and give thanks for your blessings.

Singing HU (HUUUUUU, pronounced "hue") serves as a tuning fork with Spirit that brings you into greater harmony with the Divine. We recommend singing HU a few minutes each day. This can bring love, joy, peace, and clarity, or help you rise to a higher view of a situation when upset or fearful.

1

Peace in My Heart

When facing a challenge in life it can be easy to fall into worry and lose our peace. The problem is when we lose our peace we lose our clarity too. It then becomes harder to confidently and clearly see the next step to take, which leads to more worry and uncertainty, resulting in a downward spiral. The solution is to focus on what matters most — our relationship with God. It is when we seek first the Kingdom, all things, including His peace, can be added unto us.

Have you ever wished for some peace in your heart, to have a break from worrying about what the future may bring? I was in such a situation a few years ago when I was looking for a new job. I had attended college classes at night one year after another so I could be licensed for a new career as a teacher. Then there was a window of opportunity to find a job while the spring hiring season lasted, and there was stiff competition for jobs in the area where I live. I was starting to feel stressed about the prospect of moving to a different county or significantly increasing the length of my daily commute should I not find a job close to home. Every weekend was time when I could be writing a cover letter or completing an application, but today there was an opportunity to do something different. I had a chance to sing HU with friends of mine at a nearby conference center. This was something I did not want to miss.

At the conference center the large group gathered and sang HU for a while. The beautiful sound of many voices singing together reverberated throughout the room. We sat in silence once we stopped singing, and I was immersed in gentle waves of Divine love. I then became aware of a blessing that was within the love. I recognized it as the peace of the Lord. The peace set my mind at rest and my heart at ease. It was not the same as the peace I had experienced relaxing in the shade after a day of work in the hot sun or going fishing alongside a mountain stream while on vacation. I had experienced that sort of peace as a young man, but it often would leave me when it was time to go back to school and, as I grew older, when it was time to be back at work on Monday morning. This peace was deeper. As it filled me, I was freed to be content in the moment with no concern about what the future might bring or whether I would find a new job. It was peace from the Divine; a precious gift I was intent on cherishing as long as I could.

I was also gifted with clarity. I could see clearly how when I feel myself start to lose peace in my heart it is essential to look at the direction I am heading in; I might be heading in a direction that is not where my heart is leading me. I knew in such a situation I would want to put the brakes on, listen more intently to the inner guidance within me, and be willing to change course if need be. I knew I did not want to do anything that would take me away from this beautiful, peaceful state I was dwelling in.

When the group had an opportunity to share our experiences from the HU Sing, I was amazed by the incredible variety of blessings that were shared. Each person who shared their experience had received a blessing that was tailor-made and unique for them. When I had the chance to share, I said I had been blessed with peace in my heart. Del, who was hosting the event, responded by saying how God knew what I was going through as I searched for a new job, and how I needed some peace. I left the conference center feeling happy, refreshed — at peace with myself and the world around me.

The gift I received is one that keeps on giving. Years later I have revisited the experience of the HU Sing and have been blessed by remembrance of how I do not want to do anything that causes me to lose peace. Remembering my experience helps me to have clarity about decisions I am faced with today and to choose wisely. The day at the conference center is one in a long string of blessings throughout the years. There have been many other times since the HU Sing when I have sung HU and the Divine has responded by giving me exactly what I needed. I am so grateful and continue to be amazed our prayers are heard.

Written by Roland Vonder Muhll

2

God's Guidance Leads to Abundance

*Our books contain countless stories which demonstrate the blessings that come from following nudges —
those subtle knowings and insights from the inner Prophet. When we learn to follow this guidance our life becomes more abundant, often answering the prayers of our heart — whether we've voiced them aloud or not. The following is a classic example.*

When I first graduated college I worked several jobs to earn income, but none fulfilled what I was ultimately looking for. I did not yet have a clear picture of my ideal career, but I knew a lot of the various characteristics I wanted my job to have. I had an idea of what kind of job format and environment I would thrive in but did not yet know what job would have those characteristics. I had two main career interests: exercise physiology, which was my area of study in college, and a passion for filmmaking that was just a hobby at the time. I knew ultimately I would love to be a professional filmmaker but had no practical idea of how to move forward toward that goal.

During this time period of looking for the right job, but not knowing quite what it was yet, we had a big storm that brought over a foot of snow. Living in Virginia a snow like this was a big deal. As soon as I woke up that morning I felt a strong inner knowing that I had to get up right away and go outside to check out the snow. I have learned over the years attending Guidance for a Better Life retreats these inner nudges are blessings from God, delivered through the inner Prophet. Following these nudges has helped me both avoid major pitfalls in life and also be led to really beneficial outcomes. I have learned it is always in my best interest to listen to these nudges even if I do not necessarily know the reason why.

Trusting this nudge, I walked out into the beautiful freshly fallen snow with no real objective in mind but to enjoy it. I then felt another nudge to go check out the park across the street where kids were sledding and lots of people were enjoying the snow. When I got there I saw the local news station had a crew out filming the snow day fun. After watching for a few minutes, I received another nudge to introduce myself to them and see if they might have any openings for cameramen at the news station. The reporter was excited I asked because they had that exact position to fill, and they were shorthanded until they filled it. The reporter then saw to it that my application made it to the boss's desk, with a personal referral from her, which got me an interview.

Not knowing much about this job going into it, other than I would get to use a camera every day at work, it turned out to be exactly the perfect job for me at that time. I am no longer at that job but for the year and a half I was, it was absolutely perfect for me. The job ended up fulfilling every single one of the characteristics I wanted in a job. I wanted a job with a level of creativity, that had a good amount of variety, an opportunity to interact with many different people, and was overall a fun and enjoyable way to earn a living. It turned out to be all of these things and more. I do not recall ever having an official prayer about this, but it was such a gift God heard what I wanted in my heart and set up the absolute perfect job for me at that point in my career as a filmmaker. It gave me the experience I needed to go on to start my own video production business, which is what I do now. What may have seemed like a simple nudge to go outside was anything but. It was guidance from God helping me to have a more abundant life. I could not possibly have planned it better myself even if I had tried.

Prophet Del Hall has taught me how to recognize and develop this inner communication with the Divine. It is a sacred gift and a lifeline that helps me in countless ways every day. God loves each of us and cares about us so much that He wants every part of our lives to be better. It is not only guidance on things that might be classified as major life-changing events, but even in countless smaller ways to help my day go smoother. It is such a blessing to not have to stumble through life alone. To know this inner guidance is available to all of us and can be cultivated and strengthened with the help of Prophet is such a gift. Recognizing and following Divine guidance can help us live the best life God has intended for us.

Written by Sam Kempf

3

I Held Her in Heaven

We all, as Soul, live many many lifetimes. During our earthy incarnations we develop love connections with other Souls, and often we are blessed to reincarnate with the same Souls to continue our journey together. The following is a beautiful story of a mother-to-be meeting her future daughter in the inner spiritual worlds, before her physical birth.

I have a daughter who is nearly two and a half years old. My pregnancy with her almost seems like a dream now. I can recall snippets, but mostly I remember the wondering and the waiting. A lot of that goes on in nine months. "What will she be like? Will we get along?" As first-time parents my husband and I really had no clue what to expect. While much of this time is fading from memory there is one experience I had while pregnant I will never forget. It has forever changed the way I see my daughter and the way I view our family. Prophet allowed me to meet and hold my daughter, before she was born, in Heaven.

I was five months pregnant while at a retreat at Guidance for a Better Life. This is one of my favorite places to be. As a group we sang HU and focused on sending our love and gratitude to God. In the quietude after singing HU I left my body spiritually as Soul and Prophet took me to Heaven, our true home. Each journey to this sacred place has been different. Each visit has helped me, degree by degree, to understand the tremendous love God has for me personally and for all of His creation.

This time I knelt with Prophet at the edge of God's Ocean. It was night and the water was calm. It was a gift of love from God to see it this way because there is a special beauty to me about the physical ocean at nighttime. I could feel the presence of God's Love and peace all around me and in me. I savored being in the moment experiencing the quiet stillness, like being held in a loving embrace.

Just being allowed to be here was a most incredible thing, and yet Prophet gave me another personal and sacred blessing. I looked out across the water to see a beautiful being of light emerge from the velvety depths of God's

Ocean. This being was in a female form. As the being came closer I saw she was carrying something, and to my surprise it was the Soul that would be my future daughter, Camille. The beautiful being stood in front of me holding this precious Soul in her arms, as one would cradle a cherished baby. Camille was made of God's Light and Sound. The way she moved in this being's arms was the same as in my womb, as though bursting to get out, a literal bundle of joy.

The being of light silently handed Camille to me with care, and I was allowed to hold her for a moment. It did not feel like my daughter and I were meeting for the first time. It was more a reunion of two Souls happy to see each other once again. I loved her and she loved me. How incredible to know the Soul being born into my family was indeed a Soul I had known and loved before. I was speechless. To be here in Heaven was amazing in itself, but I was also being reunited with a Soul that was to be my future daughter. Now I was even more excited and could not wait for her to be born. I could not wait for the moment when she, Soul, would animate her physical body; the moment when she would take her first breath of life in this world, and I could kiss her sweet face.

Then I gave her back to the being of light who returned into God's Ocean. I was filled with wonder and appreciation that God allowed us to meet in this sacred place. Soul, being eternal, is ageless, yet I was allowed to meet her in the form she would be taking in her new physical embodiment, that of my daughter. In this way I could hold her as I was so longing to do. This was a stunning gift from God.

Being allowed to meet my daughter before she was born into this life taught me more about the remarkable love God has for each Soul. I learned that Soul is a child of God whose true home is in Heaven. Our sons and daughters are not randomly selected, but are given to us with purpose by God's loving design. It does not matter if we are born into a family or adopted. Our families are part of a love story that started before this lifetime and will continue into future lives. In His timing God will reconnect us with our loved ones again.

I am so grateful that Camille joined our family and that I can love her again. She is such a delight! I look forward to the day when I can share with her the story of how I held her in Heaven.

Written by Carmen Snodgrass

4

Something's Not Right, Do Not Leave

God communicates with our "heart." If we choose to disregard these gentle whisperings and instead follow what seems logical, we can miss a gift of love and protection God had intended for us. Learning to trust and follow Divine guidance takes practice, but with it comes great reward.

I was in the process of moving and had a trailer load of belongings that needed to go to my storage unit in Virginia. The weather was beautiful for traveling, the trailer was loaded, and all items were covered and secured. I was anxious to get the five-hour trip started. I said to myself, "Daylight is being wasted, let's go." But something inside me said, "Do not go!"

I have learned to listen to these nudges, feelings, and that little voice inside. Yet I really really wanted to get on the road. There was no

19

logical reason for not leaving; conditions and the timing for missing heavy rush hour traffic were perfect. Everything was fine: the trailer was connected properly, the cover and tie-down straps were secure, and spare tires, lights, and fluids were in the truck; all checked out. Something still did not feel right. It was about time for a new set of front brake pads to be installed on my truck. Maybe that was what was bothering me.

I called a friend and took the truck to his garage. We installed the new brake pads and he had me pump the brake pedal several times. On the third pump the pedal went to the floor. My friend yelled to let off the brake pedal. One of the brake lines blew apart. My truck had no braking capabilities. Oh my God. Instantly, I knew God was protecting me and the people that would have been traveling near my truck and trailer. I prayed and thanked God for the feeling not to go and for His protection and guidance. Had I kept to my agenda of leaving when I wanted and not listened to the feeling, there would likely have been a terrible accident. Who knows on which steep hill or highway the brake line would have failed or how many other people in vehicles would have been in the vicinity. God knew. All that needed to be done was listen to and follow His guidance.

Several days later with new brake lines, me, the truck, and trailer load of belongings arrived safely in Virginia. There is another layer of God's protection here. The brake line burst at my friend's garage, not out on the highway or some back road. How safe and convenient that was. Because I followed God's nudge — stress, fear, panic, and worry were all avoided. My trusted and knowledgeable mechanic friend was even able to give me a ride home from his garage. Had I been on the road traveling there would have been time spent waiting on a tow truck and the repair, towing fees, a possible hotel stay, the uncertainty of finding a qualified mechanic, the cost of the brake line repair, and worrying about my safety. All of this was avoided by listening to and following God's guidance. Thank you God for your love and protection.

Written by Rebecca Vettorel

5

Mom's Loveseat

*There are times when we are not fully aware of the
hurts and angers we carry. Whether seen or unseen
they can still affect us in many ways. Ultimately, they
hold us back spiritually by reducing our ability to give
and receive love to our fullest potential. When truth is
shined on the hurt, healing can begin.*

I miss my mother. I am sure many, like me,
continue to experience the emptiness and loss of
a parent even after time passes and we ourselves
grow older. My mother did not play a big part in
my early childhood years. Most of my childhood
memories are of outdoor adventures with my
three older sisters as we explored the rural
countryside with other neighborhood kids. I have
very few early memories of my mother, and as a
young child I was never really quite sure of her
love. Demonstrating love for one another in our
family was not something that was done.
However, later in life as my mother and I grew
older we developed a friendship based on love

and a closeness that comes from being able to share with one another; oftentimes the only requirement was the other just listen. I miss our conversations.

This past spring, while attending a weeklong spiritual retreat at Guidance for a Better Life, Prophet Del Hall suggested the group ask for inner guidance and clarity on anything that may be holding us back on our journey home to God. We were to do this before going to bed for the night. Early the following morning, as I lay quietly in bed barely awake, thoughts of my mother poured in. During this quiet morning time Prophet helped me recognize I was angry at my mother because of my childhood doubts of her love for me.

Prophet's loving guidance showed me it was not that my mother did not love me as a child, it was that she herself carried scars from her childhood that prevented her from fully accepting and demonstrating love. This recognition was a blessed healing freeing me from the anger I carried and had not been fully aware of. In his Divine wisdom Prophet knew even a "little" anger was enough to hold me back from growing spiritually and continuing on my journey home to God.

I now cherish more than ever the love and friendship my mother and I developed in later years. As the weeks passed I recognized I had a prayer in my heart to tell her how much I love and miss her and to forgive her for those early childhood years. This prayer in my heart was answered on April 30, my mother's birthday! One of my first thoughts upon awakening that morning was, "Happy Birthday Mom." Later in the day I was drawn to sit in my mother's loveseat, which I had acquired after her passing and now was in a spare bedroom of my house. Sitting in Prophet's loving presence, I recalled all the cherished hours of loving conversations I had with my mother in her loveseat. The cherished conversations we had together in this "loveseat" are what had brought us closer together in friendship and love in our later years.

As I sat, I slowly became aware of my mother sitting beside me. I did not physically see her, but in that moment I definitely felt her loving presence. With joy in my heart and much emotion I talked to her. Sharing my feelings, I poured my heart out, crying and expressing to her how I missed her, loved her, and forgave her for those early childhood years. I asked her for forgiveness for the anger I had been carrying towards her. Peace descended on me as I sat in her "loveseat" and physically felt the weight of her arm come around my shoulders in a loving embrace. The prayer in my heart was answered!

By the Grace of God I am blessed by Prophet with this incredible, loving, healing experience.

Written by Donna Hospodar

6

I Took a Step and God Responded

Life has a way sometimes of nudging us towards what is truly important — a personal relationship with God. When we take steps to draw closer to Him, God does respond. The resulting relationship is what brings true peace, love, and happiness into our life.

Like so many people, I was married, had kids, a house, and my own business. By the time I reached my early forties I experienced a financial setback, the marriage failed, and my wife and I went through a rough divorce.

I left the marriage with nothing but my clothes in two suitcases. I moved into a tiny studio apartment consisting of a bedroom, a kitchenette, and a bathroom. It was in a basement with two tiny windows that did not let in any sunlight. The apartment was dark and dreary, pretty much how I was feeling at the time.

It was so small my three kids could only stay over one at a time when they visited.

Fortunately I still had my business as an appliance repair technician. One day I was at a customer's home and after fixing her washer we got to talking. Since I have had the business for many years my customers got to know me well. This customer knew I had gone through a divorce. She shared that God had helped her following her own divorce and then handed me three books to take home with me. She suggested I look them over to see if one was a good fit to read at this time in my life. I got home that night and looked at the three books. I chose the one that did not have a big picture of the author on the cover. Those seemed too much in the way of a high-pressured salesman's approach and full of vanity. The one that appealed to me was a book about connecting with God and bringing Him into your life. As the weeks passed by I found the more I read the more I started communicating with God. Praying, thanking Him, and just talking to Him. This is when things started to change in my life. My attitude was also changing. I was becoming more "alive" again and could begin to imagine a bright and happy future life.

In the bank one day, while waiting on me, the teller asked if I knew anyone looking for a bright, two-bedroom apartment. I said I would be, if the price were right. I went and saw the apartment and it was perfect. It had plenty of room for me and my kids, was very sunny inside, and had a yard for us to play in. The landlord said he was keeping the rent low and affordable, which just happened to fit my budget. I moved into this bigger and brighter place, although with no furniture.

The next day my former wife's brother called me to say he had a couch and some kitchenware if I was interested. A week later my landlord bought a new kitchen table set and asked if I wanted his old one. I had just said to my son the day before that we should go to some yard sales to look for a kitchen table! Within a month I went from a nearly empty apartment to a fully furnished one. Many of the things I needed came from random people I did not know, asking me if I knew of someone who could use these things. Some may call these coincidences, but I know in my heart these were gifts of love from God.

Years have passed, and the gifts are still coming. God is a big part of my life now. I communicate with Him daily, especially to thank

Him for my abundant life of peace, love, and happiness. In sharing this with you, the reader, my hope is that it inspires you to take the first step and invite God into your own life. You have nothing to lose, yet so much to gain.

Written by Steven Lane

7

Prune and Nourish

Balance in life is a moving target. Knowing when or where to cut back and where to let things develop is an art form. One that is much easier to do when one remains spiritually nourished.

On the night of May 22, 2015 I snuggled comfortably into my sleeping bag at Guidance for a Better Life, where I was attending a spiritual retreat. As I settled in I prayed and thanked God for the privilege of being in this sacred place again. I asked for a dream that would teach me whatever I needed next for my spiritual growth. Then I silently sang HU, a love song to God, for a few moments and soon fell asleep. That night I was given two dreams that seemed unrelated at first.

In the first dream Prophet was showing me roses on a rose bush. He was helping me decide which ones to prune to enable more vigorous growth and beauty to develop. In the second dream, he showed me a railroad track extending out in front of me. I was on the right track, but he showed me some of the railroad-ties were deteriorated and could cause a derailment. When I woke up I felt surrounded by his love. I knew these two dreams were gifts of love, though I was not yet clear on what they meant.

As God's Prophet, Del is able to teach us in the outer physical world as well as in the inner spiritual worlds through dreams and other spiritual experiences. I prayed for Prophet's help in understanding these two dreams. In contemplation he showed me the roses in the first dream represent things in my life that can be pruned away to make room for more abundant growth. This reminded me of something Prophet had taught me before, "If it does not pay rent, get rid of it!" This may include activities, relationships with certain people, habits, or anything else I allow to be a part of my life that is not in my best interest. This can change over time. What was perfect for me in the past may no longer be the best use of my time and energy. Prophet was showing me in the dream that he would help me examine what I am currently involved in and help me prune away what may be holding me back in life.

Prophet also taught me it is essential to replace whatever has been pruned with something positive, something more in line with my priorities in life. If I neglect to consciously choose an uplifting alternative, something else can by default fill that void of time and energy. If I am not careful, what slips into that void might be just as bad as, if not worse, than what was pruned away.

There are also times in life when one is involved in something that comes to an end, freeing up time and energy. For example, my elderly mother had recently passed away. Over the previous two years I had spent many hours taking care of her as she became more dependent. My brothers and I were now completing the settling of her estate and I was given these dreams just when I needed them. God's timing is perfect. Prophet was reminding me it was time to choose wisely how to spend that newly available time and energy. I am so grateful Prophet knows me better than I know myself!

This leads into the second dream. With the imagery of deteriorated railroad-ties, Prophet was showing me I had been neglecting to spend enough time and energy in doing the spiritual exercises that nourish me as Soul. This spiritual nourishment or "daily spiritual bread" must be consistently maintained day by day, like railroad ties under a track, to give a solid foundation for moving forward. In the dream Prophet was showing me if I did not do something to stay more nourished I was headed for a potential train wreck.

I began to invest more of the precious time I gained from the pruning into more focused prayerful contemplations with Prophet; singing HU to God together, studying spiritual scriptures together, and serving God with him in ways he leads me to serve. The Love of God coming through Prophet provides the spiritual nourishment. It is up to me to put forth the effort to partake of it. These are things I love to do, and doing them with Prophet is part of maintaining the strong foundation that helps keep me on track in life.

I am so grateful to Prophet for these two dreams and for his help with understanding the life lessons contained in them — prune and nourish. He is helping me have a life filled with more joy, peace, wisdom, and love. More importantly, these Divine gifts are also helping me build a closer relationship of love and trust with him. This relationship with God's Prophet is the key to an abundant life.

Written by Paul Harvey Sandman

8

Lights On, Not Lights Out

It is one thing to believe you are eternal and will carry on after the end of this physical life. It is quite another to know this truth beyond any shadow of a doubt. This knowledge not only will set you free but other Souls in your life too.

I recently was visiting my mom for a few days, and we were staying up late one night catching up. We are very close and always have interesting conversations that cover many different topics. On this particular night I sensed there was something off; she just was not herself. I asked her if she was all right, and she confided she had been feeling depressed. When I asked if she knew why, she mentioned a few possible causes, but I had the distinct feeling we were not getting to the root cause.

I asked the inner Prophet for help as we spoke, praying for Divine guidance on how I might be able to be a blessing to my mom. I was given a strong nudge to ask her if she was afraid of dying. Her reaction was very strong. She admitted not only was she afraid of dying, she had been feeling lately as though her life was already over, which was robbing her of any day-to-day peace and joy. She said in the past she had believed more in the possibility of Heaven and an afterlife, but as she was getting older she had started to seriously question it and wondered if it would just be "lights out" when she passed away.

I looked her in the eyes and told her very emphatically that she would absolutely go somewhere very beautiful, and I knew this beyond a shadow of a doubt. I told her she would see her relatives again. I reminded her that the "earth suit" she was wearing is only temporary, and as Soul, a Divine spark of God, she is eternal, and that is the real her. I told her how much God loves her. I told her where she was going was brighter and more splendorous than anything on Earth she could imagine. I said it would not be "lights out" at all — on the contrary, it would be "lights on!"

I feel she really got it. I saw her body language completely change. I saw and felt relief sweep through her. She seemed like she knew she was hearing truth. She told me the reason she believed me was because she could tell I really knew it. She asked me how I was so sure. I told her over the course of many years at Guidance for a Better Life, and with Prophet's loving guidance, I had been shown my true eternal nature. I had had many opportunities to experience myself as Soul, free of my body and earthly attachments, to the point where I know it is absolutely real.

I then once again reminded her of HU, an ancient and healing love song to God, which is available to anyone to "tune in" to their Divine nature and experience themselves more as Soul. I told her singing HU would be a great way for her to reconnect with her eternal self and identify less with her fears. I explained that the more she realized and identified with herself as Soul, the less she would fear death. We then had an opportunity to sing HU together, which is a gift I am truly grateful for.

What has occurred in the time since then, simply put, is a miracle of God. My mother experienced and continues to experience a renaissance in her life. Instead of sitting around thinking her life is over, she is out living it. She is looking forward to the future. Her depression has all but disappeared. She told me for the first time in a long time she is truly happy to be alive. And I know it was God's Love that turned the situation around.

There is a difference between believing and knowing, and knowing makes all the difference. Truly knowing you are Soul, deep down, is deeply liberating. I know I am Soul, that God loves me, and there is a Heaven. And the conviction in that knowledge not only frees me, it helped me to free someone else whom I love dearly.

Written by Laurence Elder

9

The Blue Star Before Me

❦

As Soul you can safely leave your physical body before the end of this earthly life to visit the Heavenly worlds of God. During these journeys you may even have the opportunity to meet with Prophet spiritually (who may appear as a blue star) to shed light on your past and help you live a fuller today.

One evening at Guidance for a Better Life many years ago I had one of my first spiritual experiences. My teacher, Prophet Del Hall, suggested we ask God to show us love in some way which would be appropriate for us. I headed to my tent when class was dismissed and prepared myself for bed. Shortly after going to sleep I awoke in my spiritual body.

I was outside of my tent lying on a large piece of flat mountain rock with my wife Shanna. We were both in our Soul bodies made of shimmering light. I thought I was in my physical body at first glance because everything looked the same, it was so real. The stars were crystal clear in the night sky and the moon shined brightly. As I gazed at the shimmering stars above me, a holographic three-dimensional image of a blue star emerged before my eyes. When the star appeared a feeling of great peace and love began to build within me. It started in my heart and elevated up into my eyes. I could not touch this blue star, but I tried because it looked so real. It was not within my mind's eye but outside of it. As I reached for it my hands went through the image and I waived them in front of my eyes several times. I then recalled how earlier in class Del had shared that the inner presence of God's Prophet can come as blue light. I knew the blue star was Prophet's presence, showing me God's Love as I had asked to be shown before bed. The inner Prophet was introducing himself to me and I felt so much love coming from him.

As we gazed into the night sky, in what seemed to be a dream in which I was awake, Shanna and I began a discussion about a past life we had together. We were just casually talking about this life where we both knew each other. She was sharing with me how much she loved trains, and how she liked a particular

Christmas ornament on top of our tree in that lifetime. Enough detail was given that I found out we were young brothers around the ages of nine and twelve, and she died unexpectedly from typhoid fever at twelve years old. We were both sick at the same time but I recovered and she did not. As we were talking I felt a surge of emotion and a sensation of heaviness near my chest, like a mix of sadness and illness.

I realized as a gift of love Prophet had taken me out of my physical body and allowed me to experience myself as Soul. Prophet showed me what it would be like to not have a physical body, perhaps like upon the time of death. He showed me it is possible to travel spiritually and come back to the physical body without dying. I experienced myself as Soul, my eternal self, which had no fear of death. I do not view death the same after this experience because I was shown we do not really die, and love does not die.

Shanna and I have been reunited in this lifetime, and the revelation of this was deeply touching and healing. If you have ever had someone pass on to the other side before you do, it can be very sad. Even if you believe you might see them again the pain can stay with you.

In my case it was still with me from a couple hundred years ago. Sadness I was carrying, which I was not even consciously aware of, lifted from me and also any fear or concern about death in general. I woke up from this spiritual experience renewed. I thought God must love us very much if He would give us a spiritual guide capable of sharing love and truth in precisely the right way for us. I looked out at the retreat center property just before awakening into my physical body and everything was tinted with white light. I felt I was being shown purity, like I had found something I had wanted deeply for a very long time. Del taught us that a blue star or flash of blue light was often the "calling card" of the Prophet. It was a way he could show himself spiritually to his loved ones. I felt the manifestation of the blue star was a special way Prophet introduced himself to me in this lifetime. He gave me an experience tailor- made for me.

Remembering this experience brings joy to my heart and reminds me of God's Love for me and my eternal bond with Prophet. He reunited me with a Soul I love very much and gave me a special experience I will always cherish.

Written by Tash Canine

10

Our Beloved Dog

Life is full of tough decisions, especially when it comes to our beloved pets. It is truly a gift of love from God to receive the clarity we need to move forward confidently without worry or regret. To know we have gotten the message from God and are doing the right thing brings peace during these difficult times.

The gravity of some choices can weigh heavily on a person's heart, as this one did on mine. In the spring of 2016 our dog and cherished family member, Angel, suffered a sudden traumatic brain episode that left her unable to move or discern which end was up. Her excellent health and puppy-like vigor just prior to this episode weighed in favor of her likelihood for recovery. Proving this out would involve extensive tests, along with a one or two week stay in the hospital's intensive care unit. During this time the doctor explained Angel would either show signs of a rebound and regain partial function or experience no improvement at all. The only other option was euthanasia.

One of the hardest choices an individual or family must face is an end-of-life decision for a beloved furry friend. Having had several dogs over the years, I had been charged with making such a decision more than once. I am not here to tell you it gets any easier. Stress often comes with the territory, but the emotional wear and tear can be lessened with help from the Divine. The decision before us was not one my husband and I took lightly. I was especially attached to Angel and loved her dearly. Her presence served as a daily reminder for me to pause and appreciate so many of the ways God's Love was evident in my life. Hardly a day went by that this sweet soul in a little dog's body did not make me smile, warm my heart, or help fill me with gratitude and love for God. The thought I may have already spent my last day with her made my heart ache with sadness. In my experience the presence of strong emotions can make it difficult to figure out what to do, or not do. I did not want to be led by my feelings or make a decision I might later look back on and wish I had done differently. Above all, I wanted what was best for this soul, if only I could gain clarity about what it was!

After the medical staff left us alone to ponder

the options, my husband and I closed our eyes and reached out to God inwardly for His guidance through the sacred song of HU. Just as my lips moved to utter the prayer in my heart for clarity, the entire facility went dark, and for a moment the world around us fell utterly still and completely silent. Seconds later the lights came back on and the center was again bustling with activity. A staff member poked her head in to check on us, and from the look on her face it seemed she was a little surprised to find us in such a peaceful state, having just opened our eyes. God had heard our prayer and answered it in a form we could relate to instantly: "Lights out!" And with that, we both knew it was time to let our little friend go. We also knew, just as the light and life had resumed in the medical center that evening, so too would the light and life of this soul continue.

It was not easy to let Angel go, but the clarity and reassurance we received allowed us to proceed in this direction with confidence. Looking back, the peace that came from knowing our decision was Divinely guided allowed me to move on with a grateful heart and no regrets.

Written by Sandra Lane

11

The Love of Life

Life is short; a reality that sinks in more with every passing year. Do not let fear keep you from embracing the gift of life while you have it. You do not have to be careless or foolish about it, but get out there and follow your dreams, even if it means stretching a little past your comfort zone. When you stretch — you grow, and when you do something that opens your heart it brings you closer to God.

As I stepped out over the wall and onto the pit, the reality of what I was about to embark upon really sank in. This was happening. It was no longer an idea, a plan, or a bucket list item. I already wore my helmet and neck protection as an attendant led me to sit on the wall to await my turn. This was really happening. I was about to climb into a real racecar on a NASCAR track with a professional driver and ride for six laps at one hundred and seventy miles per hour. I was about to go on my first ride-along.

At a recent retreat Del suggested I try a ride-along to help me find my love for life. It is easy to fall into a routine and create a life you like, but do not love. You find a few things you enjoy for fun, your favorite route to work, your favorite chair, or your favorite dish at the local restaurant. Unless we stretch and explore, that list tends to get smaller and smaller over time. Mine had become very small and tight. I went to work and came home to my cat, books, and television. Fun things like hiking became less and less frequent. I would hear about something like the NASCAR ride-along, and while it sounded like fun, I would dismiss it as something I would never do. It was too far, too expensive, or just not the kind of thing I did. I had my box of "things I do," and this was way outside of it.

It was time. Another attendant walked me out to await the car. Yellow car number sixteen pulled up, engine growling with a power my Subaru only dreams of. With help, the previous rider climbed out of the window. Now me. As instructed I sat on the door, put one leg in after another, and twisted down into the seat. Holy crap. I was sitting in the passenger seat of a real racecar. This would never be mistaken for a streetcar. Only that which was necessary for speed remained, my familiar comforts were nowhere to be found. The raw power of this car was palpable in the sound of the engine, the feel of the seat, all I saw around me. It was the wild beast next to my tame, domesticated car — a lion to my kitty cat.

My driver greeted me and I told him I wanted to go really fast, just in case there was any misunderstanding. I was not sure if they backed off sometimes and I wanted the full experience, as fast as he would go. He said, "Be careful what you wish for," and we were off.

Though I am not a car girl or a NASCAR fan, the sound of that engine has stayed with me. The deep, rough, roaring growl told me how powerful it was and how fast it could go. We headed towards the first curve out of the pit, gaining speed all the way. Then onto the straightaway getting faster and roaring into the next curve so fast that it pressed me into the seat, barely able to move my head. The wall was very close, but I knew I was in good hands with my driver at the wheel. I loved the pure speed in the straightaway and the intensity of the curves that made the reality of the speed very clear. We raced past all the other cars on the track, brave Souls driving a racecar possibly for the first time.

Six laps go by fast. I looked around at the other cars, the empty stands, and the track open before us. I wanted to savor each moment, each lap, each breath. It was over too fast, but I would not want it any other way. The things we enjoy always seem to be over too soon, even if they are not at one hundred and seventy miles per hour. I thanked the driver for an awesome ride and climbed out with a smile that felt as if it might split my face if it got any bigger. The attendants ensured I did not wander off onto the track in a daze of joy and speed.

The world is wide and deep with so much to experience. God did not create a dull, boring world for us to live in. It is wild and vibrant with so much wonder to offer from expansive landscapes to the delicate detail of a flower, the roar of a NASCAR engine to the whisper of falling snow, mountain peaks to ocean's depth. On the way to the track my friend had looked out at the fall leaves that graced the rolling hills and said, "God did not have to make them beautiful. He could have just had them turn brown or all the same color, but He did not. He painted the fall landscape in yellow, red, and orange. He made it beautiful for us to enjoy as He made the world so full of possibilities."

Each day and each breath is a precious gift from God. It is sad to live a grey life in His vibrant creation. It is easy to make excuses. I don't have time. It's too expensive. I'm just too busy, maybe next year. Life goes by fast too, racing towards the next sunset. There is much to see, to do, and to experience in this beautiful world. God did not intend for us to live a life that is merely fine but to love life and embrace it with gusto. Thank you Prophet for the gift of this experience and the opportunity to love life!

Written by Jean L. Enzbrenner

12

Prayer Answered, Not a Coincidence

We miss an opportunity to be grateful when we label a prayer that has been answered as a mere "coincidence." It is not about God needing credit; it is we who benefit when we recognize the Hand of God in our lives.

God knows our hearts better than we do, and many times throughout the day we are unknowingly the beneficiaries of His Love and Grace. I have had the amazing fortune to experience this in many ways through many years of going to the Guidance for a Better Life retreat center and being taught by Prophet Del Hall III. I would like to share a recent experience that touched me and what was in my heart, and also touched some of those I love in a very timely manner.

To give a little background, my fiancé's father has been challenged with some health struggles throughout the last several years, which has been a growing concern for his family and loving wife of more than fifty years. He recently took a fall at home that landed him in the hospital for several days. During that time the knowing that had been lying beneath the surface now came out into the open for his wife and family to face; it had become a serious safety risk for him to live at home. As the reader, I am guessing you can imagine the heartache and emotional distress of knowing someone you dearly love as a spouse, parent, grandparent, or friend is entering a new chapter in life that affects them and the lives of those who love them. His dear wife was faced with making a very hard decision to assure his safety and welfare. He now needed a professional environment to monitor his well being and focus on his medical care. A search was done and an assisted living facility was found that seemed suitable for my fiancé's dad, although the family was still nervous about their choice.

During this time I had prayed for him and for his family to find clarity and comfort, while leaving it open for what was God's will. I have been taught God hears every one of our prayers — those whispered to Him and those unspoken in our hearts. He answers them in His way and time. The following story is an experience in which I witnessed this firsthand.

I work at a local hospital as the Volunteer Services Coordinator. One day I was facilitating a new volunteer orientation. The orientation process requires new volunteers to complete an array of documents. Before each new volunteer leaves, I individually look over all the documents to verify their completion. I returned to my office to complete the paperwork process and found I had missed a major document's completion by one of the new volunteers. I would have to ask her to return to the hospital and finish it. The volunteer's appointment with me coincided with the time line of filling out and completing documents for the new living location for my fiancé's father. The processes and transition for his wife and family was difficult, to say the least.

The new volunteer came in for her appointment. This timely meeting was full of blessings. It gave me an opportunity to finalize her volunteer role and discover an additional volunteer opportunity that was in her heart to fulfill. I had a nudge to accompany her to the hospital to get her volunteer badge. As we were making conversation she mentioned her father and his later life health journey. Her father had taken a very bad fall at home. He broke his hip and it was determined living at home was beyond the care her mother and family could provide; it was no longer safe. Her father settled into the same assisted living facility that my fiancé's dad was going to. She explained very enthusiastically the experience and care her father received was exceptional. He and the family had a great experience with the care, staff, and environment of this assisted living facility. She only had kind and encouraging words for this particular facility. She kept saying how her whole family was very happy with their choice of this assisted living facility! What were the chances of meeting this particular volunteer, on the same day as my fiancé's mom was completing paper work for the assisted facility, and that this conversation even came up? This was more than a coincidence; it was a gift of God's Love at the perfect time.

That evening I shared this experience and conversation with my fiancé and his words were, "That gives me comfort," which he repeated several times. Later in the evening I emailed his mother and shared the heartfelt, encouraging words and experience of the volunteer. The next day she replied that she appreciated the timely encouragement and comfort, as she was having a challenging time completing the paperwork, and still having doubts she was making the best decision for her beloved husband.

God knows precisely the right way to pass on His Love to His children. He creates the perfect circumstances, words, and timing when answering prayers. Prayers are answered in individualized and unique ways, tailor-made for all concerned. Since attending Guidance for a Better Life I have had countless experiences of recognizing the Hand of God and His blessings. You might think this was a coincidence, but from my experience and knowing in my heart, there is no denying this was a blessing and prayer answered. From the "missing" completion of a document, to the nudge to accompany the new volunteer, to the random mention of her father's situation, to the timely sharing of encouragement that my fiancé and his mother needed that night. These are all examples of God's Love and prayers being answered.

God is alive and truly cares about His children. He knows what is in our hearts, what we need, and when we precisely need it. How many "coincidences" have you experienced in your life? You might want to pause and look a little deeper. Ask God to help you see His Hand and the gifts of love tailor-made just for you and your loved ones.

Written by Renée Dinwiddie

13

A Blessed Bike Ride

*Spirit is often attempting to communicate with us,
perhaps with an insight into something that will bring
more joy into our life. Maybe it's guidance on a
decision we are trying to make, or as in this story
protection from harm. In every case the insight will
bless our lives only if we are receptive to "hearing"
it and trust enough to follow it.*

I enjoy starting my day with a love song to
God called HU, along with contemplation
afterward to listen and be receptive to the inner
presence of Prophet. I ask for guidance and try
to be in continuous communication throughout
the day. A while ago I had a nudge to start riding
a bicycle. I felt this suggestion was an answer to
a prayer to find a fun outdoor activity. I go to the
gym sometimes for exercise but wanted to be
outside more often. I had played tennis most of
my life but finding an opponent to play with
around work and domestic obligations was not
easy to do regularly. I live in a beautiful place

with Appalachian Mountain views, orchards, and winding country roads, perfect for a scenic ride on two wheels.

I decided to buy a bicycle. Riding a bike can be dangerous, even on backcountry roads. You have to look out for other vehicles and make sure to inspect all of the components before riding. I noticed my new bicycle had a rubbing sound in the chain. I took it back to the bike shop where I purchased it, and the mechanic made some adjustments. It was quiet for a few rides, but then the sound started up again. I again took it to the shop and the mechanic adjusted the chain, rear derailleur, and levers again. It seemed to be riding well after this. I rode it for another year and took it back to the shop in the spring before riding season to get a tune-up and inspection. I continued to look it over before each ride. The sound had started to come back intermittently, but I could not see anything visibly wrong so I kept riding the bike.

One weekend morning I asked the inner spiritual form of Prophet to join me for a nice long bike ride. I thanked him for his continued protection in all areas of my life. I was partway into the ride when I got a feeling not to go as far as I had planned. I also felt an inner nudge from

Prophet to not ride on the nearby steep roads where going downhill creates very fast speeds. I really wanted to go farther, but I decided to cut my ride short. I felt this was a warning. A mile away from my house on the way home, the whole gearshift and chain came loose from the back wheel. Fortunately, I was riding on a gentle uphill slope so I could easily stop and unclip from the pedals safely. I was thankful no cars were around this normally busy section of the road.

When I brought it back to the shop, the previous mechanic was not working there anymore. The new repairman said there must have been a fracture where the rear derailleur attached to the wheel, which was not visible. He said that was probably what was causing the mysterious rubbing sound. The way the components fell away from the wheel made them go into the spokes. The mechanic said I was very lucky the whole frame did not break, and I was not seriously injured. He told me when riders have this type of malfunction they typically have bad crashes and go over the handlebars. I knew something was not right with the bicycle, but I could not see what it was, and neither could the other mechanic. The bike shop gave me discounts on the new parts and free labor. I am so grateful I was not seriously injured, or even slightly injured! Thank you Prophet for your loving protection.

I am sure only the Hand of God could have connected all of these events so seamlessly. The protection I was given definitely saved me from serious injury, and if the part was going to break, it could not have broken on a better day, time, and place! I am so thankful for the spiritual tools I learned at Guidance for a Better Life, which help to continually build my sacred relationship with God and His Prophet. This allows me to live a blessed life every single moment of every single day!

Written by Tash Canine

14

More Freedom Less Worry

When we are overly attached to the decisions our loved ones make it puts a "cloud" over our love for them. They are a child of God first, and as such they will never be alone. Learning to love them in a relaxed, peaceful way will help improve your relationship.

It came as an unexpected surprise when my adult daughter decided to attend a HU Sing during her impromptu visit with us one weekend. Two weeks prior, before any of us were aware she'd be visiting, Prophet — my spiritual teacher and inner guide — appeared to me in what I can now say was a prophetic dream. In this dream he explained my daughter had contacted him about an upcoming retreat, indicating in some way she wanted to surprise me.

I felt fortunate to be among those in attendance at the HU Sing that day, and sharing the experience with my daughter made it much more special. The moment I closed my eyes and began singing HU I saw her as a baby securely cradled in the arms of the Divine. I recognized her as Soul — a beautiful, glowing bundle of light and sound. My heart overflowed with an overwhelming sense of gratitude. Different moments from her life began to play out after that, allowing me to experience each one from the perspective of knowing the Hand of God has always been with her and always will be. A higher truth was evident: Although she is my daughter in this lifetime, she belongs to God and has always been in the loving arms of her Heavenly Father. The peace and trust I felt in this moment can hardly be put into words. Being totally in the moment and aware of the Presence of God, I experienced detachment from worldly concerns of every kind. Divine love filled my heart and I felt free; free to simply love.

Prophet took me on a personal journey into the higher worlds and it changed me. The experience was tailor-made to bring me peace, trust, and a greater understanding of love, as it is in Heaven. Through this experience I was able to recognize my two grown children as adults, which has positively affected how I interact with them. I am less emotionally attached to their decisions and free of the expectations I once carried of being invited to weigh in on their decisions. I now have room to enjoy their presence and relate to them as treasured friends; precious Souls I am blessed to share this life with as we each make our way home to God.

It is a profound gift to savor the experiences of life together, unfettered by the emotional entanglements I once mistook for love. I am grateful to Prophet for showing me a higher, purer way to love, one that allows me to care in a relaxed and peaceful way.

Written by Sandra Lane

15

Greater Abundance Follows Past-Life Healing

Whether we are conscious of them or not, the things from our past affect us in the present. We can attempt to "wall off" or ignore old areas we do not wish to look at, but they are still there. When we are ready to face old issues, Prophet can help us disentangle from the things that no longer serve us.

I had a dream I was in my house. It was a multi-storied bright, sunny, and open space. Suddenly I found myself in a different part of the house I did not remember being there, or I had not been in for a long while and had forgotten about. I was on a lower level, perhaps a first floor or basement, and it was a separate structure but was attached to my house and shared a common wall. I briefly caught a glimpse of this from the exterior and then was back inside. This attached section was old and in very bad shape.

When first walking around the large rooms it looked as if it might have potential. I thought to myself maybe I could fix it up and rent it out. Then I looked up and saw the ceilings — they were near collapsing. I noticed the floors — they were torn up and debris was everywhere. It looked as if no one had lived there for awhile, with just a few remnants of former life there. It was so bad all I could think was how expensive it was going to be to fix all this. It would probably require a home equity loan, which I did not really want to do. It needed to be dealt with right away because it was a hazard. I was even afraid being in there because it was so unsafe. I was also concerned about the way it was attached to the nice, well-built home I lived in. I did not want this old section to cause it to collapse or become structurally damaged.

Then something very cool happened. I woke up while still in the dream and became conscious. This has only happened to me once or twice before that I can recall. At first I was relieved I was in a dream and not in any immediate danger. Then since I was not in my physical body and therefore not constrained by the body's physical limitations, I started trying things I may not have done otherwise, like putting my fists through the wall and jumping up high enough to go through the ceiling and punch into it. I was covered in dust and plasterboard but knowing it would not collapse on me physically gave me a sense of freedom and boldness to try such things. I realized this dilapidated structure was beyond repair and had to be demolished. I think this was my way of getting things started. I was very concerned when I awoke however, because houses sometimes represent one's state of consciousness when they show up in dreams. Prophet was trying to get my attention to help me, so I asked him for help in understanding the dream he blessed me with.

After a few contemplations and looking at it from different perspectives, he helped me see some pearls contained in the dream. I was excessively attached to something from the past, and it was negatively impacting this life. Perhaps this was not in an overt or easily noticeable way but in a fundamental (structural) way. This was symbolized by the section of house I not been in for a long time. The sunlit, multi-storied part of the home I usually lived in was positive, but this older attached section was bad off and potentially hazardous. The common wall between the older and newer sections suggested that not only was it something I had a hard time letting go of, there was also an attempt to keep it compartmentalized and isolated or unacknowledged. Even so, I was hurting my spiritual growth and limiting the freedom, joy, and abundance in my present life by closing my heart or trying to "wall off" this section.

This information was not totally new to me, as months prior to this Prophet had taken me back to a lifetime in the past that was probably the root of the issue. This spiritual travel experience was the beginning of a long healing process that continued with this dream. While it is true just one meeting with God's Prophet can dramatically change one's life for the better, something of this delicate and complex nature cannot be done all at once, not because he is unable to do it, but because it would have been too much for me to try and fix all at once. In Prophet's perfect, loving way, he was gently raising and expanding my awareness of the situation little by little, at a rate I could handle without being too much or putting me out of balance. All the while I was being held, loved, and protected in the Hand of God, which I was very aware of throughout.

What was significant about this dream was how clearly I saw the situation and understood. The dream spoke to me as Soul in my native language more directly and clearly than any words or mental dialogue could have conveyed while awake. What was also very significant was that I woke up in the dream, and with the boldness and confidence of Soul, I began to take an active part in taking down the old structure. It was a turning point in both understanding and accepting truth given to me by Prophet. I was ready to acknowledge it for what it was, let go of what I was holding onto, and move forward.

One morning while driving to work, shortly after this dream occurred, I saw a truck with the words "Precision Remodelers" written on the back. This awake dream caught my attention, and I knew it was a message for me. It reminded me of the house dream, and how I was concerned in the dream about how to get rid of the old rundown structure without damaging the nice part of the house. I could certainly use a "precision remodeler." I perceived a blessing and inner healing was taking place. Through this entire process that began months earlier with the initial spiritual travel experience, and even before then by conditioning and preparing me,

Prophet's precision and expertise was safely helping me dismantle the wall in my heart and attachments to the past I had been holding, without doing damage. He has made it so the love and cherished memories from that time could flow forward into the present without any of the negative baggage, for that has been let go and replaced with Divine love.

I feel I am being remodeled and upgraded in that I can feel and appreciate love in new and deeper ways. I notice it in a more honest, loving relationship with Prophet, deeper trust, and more precise inner communication with him. I notice it in more genuine and intimate connections and exchanges with friends and family. I have also noticed more Soul to Soul interactions with others I meet throughout the day. I even notice it in a deeper savoring, wonder, and appreciation for nature and in those special little moments when I experience God's Love through the world around me. It is difficult to put into words but it feels as if a shadow, one I did not even know had cast itself over my already blessed and abundant life, has been removed. I am beginning to see a richness, color, and depth of life and love I have not experienced before.

Prophet wants only the best for us and does not want us to settle for anything less than our true potential, and he knows what this is even if we do not. What was already a very nice house — a beautiful life filled with blessings upon blessings — is becoming even more beautiful, more joyful, more love-filled, and more abundant. It is sometimes hard to imagine, but there truly is always more. Anything is possible with Prophet, and with genuine love and rock-solid trust in him our growth, splendor, and potential to be a blessing to others has no limits.

Written by Lorraine Fortier

16

My "Unanswered" Prayer Was Answered

Often God will answer a prayer, but we do not recognize it because it's not what we think we want. With the blessing of hindsight we begin to see how indeed our heart's desire was fulfilled. The more we recognize this in our life the easier it is to trust, even when things go differently than we had hoped.

In 1990 Garth Brooks released a song that became a number one hit called "Unanswered Prayers." I have always been intrigued and pleasantly amused by the lyrics: "Remember when you're talkin' to the man upstairs that just because He doesn't answer doesn't mean He don't care. Some of God's greatest gifts are unanswered prayers." An unanswered prayer might lead to your wildest dreams coming true. The song describes crossing paths with an old high school girlfriend many years after graduation. He describes how each night in high school he had spent praying God would keep them together, but the relationship had not worked out. He realized when seeing her again she was not the match God had intended for him, and he thanks the good Lord for the gifts in his life, including his wife. The moral of the story always stayed with me. God can see the big picture and knows where our path may lead us long before we do. When I heard the song growing up it never occurred to me I would experience in a dream exactly what the song described.

I am blessed with an amazingly loving husband and three happy and healthy children. We recently built our dream home on family land on a beautiful mountain. God, His Prophet, and His teachings are the foundation of our lives, and I truly know I am living the life the Divine had planned for me. However, if you had asked me fifteen years ago I would have never consciously described living a life half as incredible as my current reality. God took my childhood dreams of marriage, children, and a life filled with service and knocked them out of the ballpark. One night I was given the gift of a dream from Prophet that reminded me of a forgotten prayer I had once made. I am so grateful it went "unanswered." I know all of our prayers are heard and answered in one way or another, and sometimes we have the eyes to see. In my case, God answered the true prayer in my heart, not the prayer I thought I wanted answered. Our Father knows best.

Before I went to sleep one night in January 2017 I sang HU and practiced a spiritual exercise Prophet had recently taught me. I thought of something I was grateful for specifically from that day and asked Prophet for a dream that would help me deepen my relationship with him. As I drifted off to sleep I promised to be receptive to the truth I would receive. In the dream my husband, my children, and I were at an event when we bumped into a boyfriend from my college years. He was with his current girlfriend and we greeted each other, just as stunned as we would have been in the physical after fourteen years of not seeing one another. Once our brains had time to compute who we were seeing we said hello. I introduced him to my family, and he introduced us to his girlfriend. Then came the awkward pause when the details of our last phone call returned to my consciousness while still in the dream.

Towards the end of 2003 he and I had spoken on the phone about meeting in Philadelphia in between Christmas and New Year's Eve. At that time we were no longer dating but had recently reconnected and were planning the trip to give our feelings a second chance. On the surface we seemed to be a great match, and I had said a prayer the trip would be a success. We picked a day to meet and ended the phone call with him saying that he would call me the next week to finalize plans. He never called. I remember being very disappointed and not understanding why he had not called. He had seemed excited about the trip and it did not seem like him to cancel without letting me know.

I had also planned a trip to Texas for New Year's Eve to visit a good friend and her family. That trip did come to fruition, and it was in Texas that I met a man who would become my first husband and father of my beloved daughters. I realized in the dream if I had gotten the phone call and traveled to Philadelphia, one of the most important connections in my life may not have come to be. Alas, the journey of my life continued, and after a few perfect ups and downs I was led to my current husband, and we have been blessed with a son and a beautifully abundant life.

In the dream the college beau and I stammered a bit back and forth and finally, at about the same moment, we both said something to the effect of "what happened to that trip we were supposed to take?" I said, "Well you never called so it didn't happen." He looked a bit shocked and said, "I did call. No one ever picked up and you didn't have an answering machine." In that instant in the dream the word TRUST appeared in all capital letters in my inner vision. It was like all the pieces of the puzzle or all of the unanswered questions in a movie plot clicked in my brain. He had called, and God had miraculously and graciously intercepted the call. At that time in 2003 I was living with my father and stepmother, and we definitely had an answering machine and rarely missed calls. I knew in my heart right then God had lovingly set into motion a plan he had for me. Flashing forward to 2017 I looked at my husband in the dream. I trust completely and knew it had all worked out according to Divine plan so I politely and kindly said, "Oh geez... I'm sorry that we weren't able to connect back then... but I'm glad you are doing well and it was so nice to see you." We parted ways and the dream ended.

I awoke filled with gratitude to God for lining up the life He has envisioned for me. It is very clear to me now, for multiple reasons, the young man I dated in college was not the long-term partner God had in mind for me. We have very different values and very different life goals. Ironically, he turned out not even to believe in the institution of marriage or want children. At the time it had never occurred to me to ask.

In the time since the dream I have been comforted by the deep knowingness that when we truly trust in the Divine plan and follow the whispers of our heart, everything will work out as intended. Even if something happens in life that doesn't make complete sense on the surface, remain ever peaceful and TRUST in your relationship with God. My true prayer was heard and answered by God, and I am grateful to have the eyes to see His Hand continually blessing my life. God always has a plan and as the Lord saith in Jeremiah 29:11 NIV, "I know the plans I have for you, plans to prosper you and give you hope and a future."

Written by Catherine Hughes

17

Before the Source of All

*When you recognize the Love of God is in every
aspect of your life, the little things and even the
minor annoyances look different. To actually be
taken on a spiritual journey to the source of God's
Love puts things in perspective even more. It can
inspire one to be a point of light for others so
they too may return home.*

As a student of Del Hall III, the God-ordained
Prophet of our times, I have been shown how to
recognize the many blessings in my life, to listen
to Spirit in the stillness of my heart, and to
recognize who I really am — Soul, a spiritual
being loved immeasurably and unconditionally
by God. These are keys to a more abundant life
God makes available to us through the teachings
of His Prophet. There is no disconnect between
God's Love for us whether it be at the top of the
spiritual mountain or in our daily lives. Knowing
this is comforting; experiencing it is truly special.

It was the summer of 2014. I was at our annual retreat known to students at Guidance for a Better Life as "Reunion." During the retreat we were spiritually taken by Prophet to our physical homes. I was shown the amazing amount of love there. Everything in my home and around it was a gift from God. There was my family, all our interactions, the laughter, and the love we shared. It was also in things I saw as the minor annoyances of daily life such as the messy piles of children's clothes on the floor. The piles meant there were plenty of clothes for the kids, many of which were hand-me-down gifts from a dear friend. There was a working washing machine and dryer and three beautiful children to wear the clothes. There were also many subtler gifts. I did not realize how much they touched my heart, such as the amazing view of the sunset I often admired from my porch at the end of the day. All was by God's Love and Grace. It was amazing to witness.

As I was spiritually standing in my home I was then shown the source of this love. I was taken by Prophet to the Abode of God, taken before the Source of All! Here, from everywhere and from everything, came love. It too was God's Love, the same love I experienced in my home, but on a scale that was unimaginable. It was like being so close to the sun you could not see anything that was not the sun. All of creation originated here. I was humbled and in awe. As I knelt before the Almighty I felt my capacity to love stretched beyond my comprehension. I actively received more and more, finding my innate way to gratefully accept God's Love. Prophet's spiritual presence kneeling beside me was also humbling. His teachings, guidance, and love brought me to the Source of All, yet here he too knelt in reverence. His love for me as Soul and his devotion to God inspires me daily. Appreciation overwhelmed me. I cannot put into words the gratitude I felt at that moment.

As my consciousness returned to my physical body at the retreat center, I had a nudge to open a specific book. I opened to a page of scripture that described the Voice of God traveling out from Heaven like a wave, carrying all life with it and then returning back to the Source; bringing with It those Souls ready to serve God. The paragraph resonated perfectly with my experience! As I read this, still basking in the jaw-dropping wonder of my experience, I spiritually heard another layer of insight over it, as if spoken directly to my heart: "And now we are sent out again, not in ignorance, but in knowingness; not in darkness, but as points of light; not in forgetfulness, but to remind other Souls; no longer lost in the wilderness, but to help others find you again." The words emphasized to me that as a student at Guidance for a Better Life I had received so much, experiencing the glories of God many times over — love, blessings, insights, healings, clarity, and peace. My cup truly runneth over! And now the opportunity was coming to give back in a greater measure and to share my gratitude and appreciation for God's teachings.

This experience helped me to more consciously recognize the Love of the Heavenly Father that flowed in my life. There is something special about recognizing the love in one's life and Its source. Whether it is through a child, a spouse, a pet, or a beautiful sunset — love is love. It blesses us from On High. As I look now at the view in my home I still see Heavenly Love.

With Prophet we have the ability to return to the Source. Yet God's Love is not reserved solely for the Heavenly realms. It is everywhere throughout our lives. Prophet can help us recognize the love that sits like unopened presents under the Christmas tree. It may be disguised as a messy pile of clothes, a sink full of dirty dishes, or toys strewn across the living room floor, but God's Love is there. Del has helped me to see the love and abundance throughout my life. Recognizing it on a daily basis and expressing my appreciation and gratitude for it has only made it multiply. The Prophet is here now to help those who are ready to follow the calling of their heart and witness God's Love for themselves here and now.

Written by Chris Comfort

18

Golden Gift from God

This amazing story of God keeping someone alive, until they could receive the physical medical treatment they needed, reminds us that with God and Prophet anything is possible.

A few months ago I was given a strong inner nudge to follow through on several tests that were suggested to me two and a half years previously. At that time a young, new doctor had been concerned over my pulse rate of fifty-eight beats per minute. I had difficulty convincing her that was a typical pulse rate for me. I was in between jobs at the time and felt like I would be putting out money I did not have to prove to her that, "Yes indeed, my pulse has been low all of my life and is normal for me." Now, two and a half years later I was given the nudge to complete the tests. The tests were set up through a cardiologist and included an echocardiogram and then carrying around a portable heart monitor unit for twenty-four hours. I expected the two tests would come back fine, and on I would go with my life. Little did I know listening to this nudge from the Divine may have saved my life!

Shortly after returning the monitor back to the clinic, I received a phone call saying I needed to see a specialist the next day. I began to protest and try to delay as it was difficult to get time off from work. Then the nurse started throwing numbers at me. She said my overall average pulse rate for the twenty-four hours was forty-two with a low of twenty-four, and at one point my heart had stopped for 3.6 seconds. That got my attention!

The next day I met with the specialist who said I needed a pacemaker. I was in shock. The idea of a pacemaker for me was unthinkable. All my life I have done alternative approaches to my life and health, and have always been very healthy. I took no medicine on a regular basis — there had to be a mistake. Somehow something had temporarily affected the tests, or perhaps there was something we were missing that could be identified and corrected. My pulse was thirty-seven that day at the specialist's office and he was blown away I could be sitting up and talking with him. He recommended I not wait, saying it would be important to go ahead with the pacemaker implant in the next one to three weeks. Hopefully I was going to wake up from this bad dream.

Although initially I was experiencing some extra stress, at my core I was very much at peace with the knowingness of how much I am loved by God, and that I am always in the Hand of God no matter what the outcome. But yes, I would very much like to stay here on the Earth plane at this time. I have the most amazing opportunity of lifetimes to learn and grow under the guidance of a living Prophet, both on the inner and outer. However, I also came to peace that if it were my time to move on to one of God's Heavens to serve as a coworker there instead of here, so be it; I would still be loved and in God's Hand.

Surgery was scheduled for two weeks later. Meanwhile I researched online everything I could relating to low heart rate, bradycardia, including: hypothyroid, type two diabetes, Lyme's disease, parasites, low electrolytes/minerals, etc. I really wanted a second opinion; although it felt like things were happening too quickly and there would not be time. On the inner I kept hearing Prophet say, "What are you waiting for?" I felt an urgency in Prophet's words. When I stopped to think about answering his question, I realized I did want a second opinion from another specialist. I wanted to know if this was truly the best course of action for me or were we missing something.

During a thirty-six hour period a dear friend of mine who is also tuned in to Divine guidance on the inner gently asked me at least three different times what I was doing about getting a second opinion. I was very grateful Prophet worked through him, and I decided to at least try. I called the cardiology group and was put through to voicemail for the nurse of one of the cardiologists. My inner guidance was to call again the next day and this time managed to speak to the nurse. I told the nurse I would like a consultation, a second opinion, and that time was of the essence. She explained they were booking appointments a month away, although she thought perhaps the doctor might agree to look over my paperwork if they could get it in time. However, she said it did sound like I needed a pacemaker. When I got off the phone I was a bit discouraged. The next afternoon while at work I received a miracle call! It was the nurse calling to say the doctor was willing to see me the very next morning, paperwork or no paperwork. I got off the phone crying tears of joy and thanksgiving to Prophet for this amazing gift!

As I waited for the doctor to come into the room, I closed my eyes and held hands with the inner Prophet. The door opened, and I opened my eyes to a room filled with golden light, nearly blinding me. There was golden light everywhere in the room, showering me; an overpowering sense of God's Love permeating everything. It was like waking up inside a precious golden gift personally from God, a gift of a second opinion. The doctor introduced himself and sat down next to me, seemingly with all the time in the world to get to know me and address all my questions and concerns. How often does that ever happen in the medical world? In that golden bubble of time out of time, the doctor patiently addressed every one of my questions and concerns. He drew a rough diagram of a heart and very clearly explained how the heart functions. And he showed me my EKG printout that had been taken that morning and explained what he could see in each of my heartbeats on the graph. It showed that overall my heart was doing what it is supposed to do although my heart's natural pacemaker, which is the size of a marble, was not up to speed. With my heart starting at a low pulse rate to begin with, I did not have much "wiggle room." He concurred I needed a pacemaker, and not to wait.

I walked out of the room full of joy and inner peace with overflowing gratitude for the second opinion arranged by God, highlighted by His golden Light. It was very comforting and reassuring. Also, I was very grateful for the doctor serving as an instrument for the Divine. I was completely at peace moving forward with the pacemaker implant; that was what I needed to do. My spiritual teacher Del, who is God's Prophet, has told us it is important to trust and also to verify. That afternoon on my lunch break I called Del to let him know what was going on with me. The one question he asked, "Did you get a second opinion?" Did I ever! We truly are loved way beyond our possible imagination. The prayer of my heart was heard and answered.

Since my surgery I have been very surprised to discover I feel strong with a solid foundation under me when I am walking. I realized for quite a while before getting the pacemaker my legs had been buckling out from under me, and I kept wondering why I was so out of shape. I had not made the correlation this had something to do with my heart. As the weeks passed I felt stronger with more energy and alertness, and have more "gears" working rather than going slow and slower. Being showered in God's golden Light brings an abundance of gifts, and I am grateful for this continuing gift of healing in my life.

I recall the amazement of the specialist that I was actually sitting upright with a pulse of thirty-seven. I have come to the realization and knowingness that God and Divine Spirit had been propping me up, keeping me going until I could get the medical assistance I needed. Thank you Prophet for all of your guidance, love, support, and protection.

Written by Jan Reid

19

Say What You Need to Say

Our love and gratitude for others is of its greatest value when we actually take the time to express it. It is also best to express the things that weigh heavy on our heart instead of pretending they are not there. The truth will set you and your loved ones free.

My relationship with my physical father is a loving one. I cherish him and know he loves me. He has been very supportive and generous with me throughout my life. I was seven when my parents divorced and my mother moved us back to the States while my father remained in Europe for his work. I still saw him several times a year, yet his physical absence had left a hole in my childhood. Growing up there were some walls between us in the way we related. Our conversations tended to stay on safe topics like how's the weather, what's for dinner, and what we were going to do that day. All sorts of things, particularly feelings, were not discussed and rarely addressed or acknowledged.

Over the years I accepted this was the way things were between us. Fifteen years ago he moved about three hours away from me and my family to a beautiful home near the Chesapeake Bay. I loved going to visit him and sharing our love of the outdoors. We had pleasant walks with my children around his farm and enjoyed sitting on his dock together watching the kids play in the bay. We also shared interests about projects around the house. But deep inside I wanted to share more. I tended to leave my visits feeling like something was missing; something was unsaid and unexpressed.

One Sunday a few years ago I heard a whisper from the Divine. The suggestion came in like a gentle, soothing wind, "Write your father a letter and say what you need to say." I remember the way the sunlight was beaming through my window casting clarity and warmth over the moment. So I got a pad of paper and began, "Dear Papa." I wrote it with help from the Divine, my heart pouring out through the pen onto the paper. Years before I had written a similar letter to another family member during a retreat at Guidance for a Better Life. At that retreat my teacher had suggested writing a letter of love and appreciation to someone as a healing exercise. It had been wonderfully freeing and a tremendous blessing to write. The process of writing it softened my heart, but I did not have the courage to mail it.

As I wrote this letter to my father I was experiencing a similar freedom which came from saying what was in my heart. In a way this remembrance gave me more courage to share without preconceived notions about what was the "right" thing to say. I knew my father carried regrets and worries over how his choices had affected us. By now we were both pretending the "old elephant-in-the-room" was a couch. As I wrote this letter I expressed appreciation for my childhood, even the sad part. I acknowledged how much he loved me even though our family life had not gone how he had wished. I also acknowledged our mutual pain. It became a letter of gratitude, a letter to say I really love you; a letter to reassure him I forgave him, and knew he did the best he could, and that I held no hard feelings. I also acknowledged my own shortcomings in how I had held grudges and anger as a teenager and apologized for how this had hurt him.

The Divine whisper to write my father a letter was stirring other things as I wrote. It was healing to say, "I forgive you and I am sorry." It was healing to express love without any strings attached. In expressing what was in my heart a wall had come down, and the old pain which had been tucked away inside, was let go. After I signed the letter I felt so free. I put a stamp on the envelope and mailed it. My father received it a few days later and called to express how much it had touched him. I was so happy he had accepted my love. Even in that phone call something in how we related to each other had changed. He questioned why it sometimes takes courage to truly say I love you to the people that matter most in our lives.

The following time I went to visit him with my family things were different between us. There was a softening and a closeness between us I had always known was possible. I felt complete in my relationship with him. The process of following the Divine's suggestion to write a letter led to a healing of my heart and a healing in our relationship.

A few months later my father had a stroke and was sent to the hospital. As soon as I heard the news I took a deep breath. No matter how his condition unfolded I did not have regrets with our relationship. I loved him and had expressed it. The Divine had foreseen this and gave me the opportunity to say what I needed to say, before it may have been too late to say it in the physical. Gratefully the stroke did minimal damage and my father had a full recovery. This brush with the end of his life continued our healing as we grew in our relationship. Each visit we became closer and our way of relating more genuine.

The lesson in this experience for me was that Divine whispers or suggestions are for our benefit and for the benefit of others. These Divine whisperings are gifts of love, because we are so loved by God. By following the advice to write my father a love letter, walls came down and we were able to give and receive more love with each other.

Written by Molly Comfort

20

Hidden Blessings

*Often we are not aware the Hand of God has reached
into our lives to bless, guide, or protect us. When we
do recognize these gifts of love our gratitude and
appreciation grows, which opens our hearts
even further to God's Love.*

I was working on the computer the other week
downloading files. As they were rather large files
it took some time to do the transfer. In between
keystrokes I began to contemplate on the
miracles of God and God's blessings. I was
sitting there quietly with no agenda, just thinking
about the magnificence of God's Grace.
Suddenly I received a tremendous download of
love that touched me in so many ways. A
wonderful volume of love poured into me, a gift
so precious. Thanking God's Prophet for this
wonderful gift, I thought about all the blessings I
receive from God through God's Prophet. Over
the years I have come to discover everything in

my life is a gift from God. Sitting there in my office I felt so much love, gratitude, and appreciation. My cup most certainly runneth over.

This started me thinking about the love and gratitude I have for all the gifts I recognize in my life: my family, home, friends, and the gift to see God's Love manifest in my life in so many ways. My contemplation then shifted as a new thought entered my consciousness. I considered the gifts of love God brings to me I do not recognize. Then I was reminded of an experience I had several weeks previously. I was working on a job out on the ocean near New England. The ocean weather in winter can become quite rough and unpredictable. We could only work a few days at a time before a storm would blow through, requiring us to leave our worksite and avoid the worst of the weather in a safe harbor. The one hundred foot boat we were on was well-maintained and the crew very professional. When the weather forecast called a "Small Craft Advisory" we knew to pay attention and find shelter. This particular time a storm was developing so we moved the vessel to the harbor and set anchor. The wind kept increasing throughout the day, and by nightfall we had sustained winds of fifty to sixty miles per hour and gusts over seventy miles per hour. We were still safe. The crew kept a steady watch on our situation and the weather. They had to reset the anchors several times as the wind would push the boat causing the anchors to drag on the bottom.

Going to bed I could feel the wind shifting the boat as it bobbed and rolled against the anchor and chain. Curling up in my sleeping bag I was warm and comfortable, grateful that it was so. I slept well that night. Awakening the next morning I greeted the crew in the galley. They proceeded to tell me that during the night they had recorded a wind speed of over one hundred and four miles per hour. I immediately saw the magnitude of this event, and felt like I had been part of a miracle. My heart turned to God to give thanks for the incredible protection and for keeping us all safe. To put this in perspective, a Category One hurricane has sustained winds of at least seventy-four miles per hour. Speeds as high as eighty-nine miles per hour were recorded when Hurricane Sandy moved through the Garden State. Hurricane Katrina made its second landfall as a Category Three hurricane with sustained winds of one hundred and twenty miles per hour in Louisiana. The winds we experienced were not sustained and would not be considered a hurricane, but the number of things that could have happened to our little vessel boggles the imagination. Yet there we were, sipping coffee in the morning as if nothing had happened. We were safe and secure as if we were being held in God's Hand. The storm had passed and the morning sky was amazing.

Sitting in my office in front of the computer, again safe and warm, I wondered about the countless times God has protected me, kept me and my loved ones safe from harm, steered me in the right direction at just the right time, and put the right conditions in front of me to answer the prayers of my heart. All those times and I was not aware of any of it. I can however, try my best to be more aware of and grateful for the blessings I do recognize, to be more aware of God's Presence throughout the day, and demonstrate gratitude and appreciation for God truly keeping me safe in the palm of His Hand.

Written by Paul Nelson

21

Every Day is a Gift From God

❦

An attitude of gratitude makes all the difference in life, and fortunately there is always something to be grateful about. Perhaps the greatest gift, which can sometimes be overlooked, is the gift of life itself. The small things that sometimes get us down melt away when we remember the blessing of being alive to live another day in God's Love.

Have you ever considered God gives us the exact experiences we need in life to help us know His Hand is in everything? I have been blessed by a true spiritual teacher, Prophet Del Hall III, who has helped me recognize no experience in life is simply random or coincidental. It is all a part of God's plan to help us grow closer to Him and recognize His Love is all around. I was blessed years ago when Prophet helped me recognize the gift of working with a man who showed up at my job one day.

His name was Juan, and he had recently arrived in Virginia from Honduras. He was an air-conditioning and refrigeration mechanic by trade. Due to economic problems in his home country he was now working on a landscaping crew with me and trying to save as much money as he could to send home to his family. My supervisor assigned him to work with me most days, because I was the only one on the crew who could explain the details of the job to Juan in Spanish. As we worked together for long hours in the hot summer sun, I began to see he had something precious, more precious than any American dollars: he had a grateful heart.

One hot, humid afternoon as we pruned bushes next to a busy street we began talking about the spiritual side of life. Juan was a devout Christian who spoke about the Bible and God in a reverential tone. At one point he paused and said emphatically, "Every day is a gift from God." His words went right into my heart. In that moment there was nothing to stress over. The hours of working in the summer heat, the traffic noise, feelings of loneliness since a relationship had recently come to an end, nothing that had been bothering me in days past mattered. It was a gift to simply be alive for another day with God.

While I felt Juan was speaking from his heart, I know it was also the spiritual presence of Prophet, the Voice of God, who was speaking words of wisdom through Juan in that moment.

That conversation with my friend from Honduras helped me look at life with a more grateful attitude. I went on to enjoy many more conversations with Juan as we became good friends. Many years have passed since I last saw Juan, but his words stay alive in my memory. Prophet, through his inner presence, has often taken me back to that moment when Juan expressed his gratitude for God and reminded me of what a precious gift each moment truly is.

Prophet has also shown me not only is each moment a precious gift from God, but that many of the people we cross paths with in life may also be the carriers of God's Love. One day when I was talking with Del about how I felt blessed to be able to work with immigrants like Juan and help them feel more at ease in the United States, he raised the possibility that maybe Juan was a spiritual teacher whom God had sent to me because I was the one who needed some help. He certainly did teach me about gratitude and how to keep a positive attitude at a job that was not always pleasant or easy. He did this not just by things he would say, but mostly through the example he set, often having a smile on his face and a sense of humor while he worked with enthusiasm, regardless of the weather or the task we were assigned.

I have grown to appreciate that the Voice of God, the Holy Spirit, is always communicating to us. Sometimes the communication comes to us through friends, coworkers, and seemingly random strangers, as well as from within ourselves. What a privilege it is to know there is a Prophet of God upon Earth who can teach us to hear the whispers of Spirit.

Written by Roland Vonder Muhll

22

A Gift of God's Peace

To be truly present in the moment, conscious of the inner presence of Prophet and fully aware of God's Love for you, brings a peace that surpasseth all understanding. All these gifts come from having a conscious relationship with God's Prophet, the greatest blessing of all.

I recently had the privilege of attending a one-day retreat at Guidance for a Better Life titled "Recognizing Divine Guidance." At this retreat God's chosen Prophet, Del Hall III, shared precious Spiritual Keys and tools to help us recognize Divine guidance in our lives. Prophet shared that the whisperings of God in our lives demonstrates God's Love for us. Understanding the whisperings of God helps to teach the ways of God which can "lead to a more abundant life with less road blocks or detours." On this particular day one of the ways I was blessed to recognize God's Love for me was through an experience I had during a HU Sing.

HU is an ancient name for God and love song to God. Singing HU is a beautiful way to express love and gratitude to God. Del shared that singing HU tunes a person in to the Divine and opens us to God's Love. Singing HU can raise us up to higher levels spiritually. He has also taught me that thinking of something I am grateful for in life opens my heart and is good to do before singing HU. I took the opportunity to express gratitude to God for the gift of my wife and for the blessing of being present at this retreat with Prophet and many other beautiful Souls.

As I sang HU I focused on each one as an expression of my love for God and was touched by an amazing and sacred gift: that God created Soul, our true selves, with the capacity to give and receive Divine love. As we sang HU I began to feel spiritually lighter as my heart filled with God's Love. This reminded me of Prophet sharing that singing HU "uplifts our consciousness" and "brings spiritual nourishment." Through my spiritual eye I began to perceive God's Light in white and gold colors flowing through Prophet to the group as a whole and to each person individually. I had the impression each person was receiving a personal gift of love from God through His Prophet.

During the quiet time after singing HU I was blessed with an opportunity to be with the inner presence of the Prophet. I looked into his eyes and heard the words, "Just be." Physically I felt my shoulders relax, and I cherished "just being" in this moment with Prophet. A deep peace bloomed in my heart, and I recognized this peace as a personalized gift of love from God through His beloved Prophet. This gift of peace woven from God's Love for me also brought the sense of a deeper trust in God and His Prophet. One of the pearls of wisdom Del shared during the retreat was that recognizing Divine guidance "helps build trust in God being there for you." I am incredibly thankful and blessed to know this is true from personal experience, for never in my life has this been more apparent than in recognizing, nurturing, and appreciating the sacred gift of having a conscious relationship with the Prophet of our times. I am truly grateful God always has a living Prophet here to teach us through personal experience, about our true and Divine nature as Soul and helps to guide us on our wondrous journey home to the Heart of God.

Written by Shanna Canine

23

Confident in My Decision

⁓

Our mind and emotions are part of who we are in this world, but they are not the eternal spiritual side of us. Soul is, and it is Soul that has a direct line of communication with the inner Prophet. This relationship brings us the clarity to make decisions we can have peace with instead of decisions solely based on emotions.

My sister and I live several hundred miles from one another and seldom have the opportunity to spend time together as we once did. As a gift for my forty-ninth birthday she invited me to travel as her guest on a trip out West — a trip that would involve meeting one another at a connecting airport before traveling to our final destination. As much as the thought of having this time together appealed to me, I did not want to jump into it blindly.

An aspect of my spiritual education at Guidance for a Better Life has taught me the importance of maintaining balance in all areas of my life, and that doing so goes hand in hand with living an abundant life. Few things threaten our balance more than allowing our emotions to dictate our decisions. And while the mind is a useful tool, Soul, our true Self, resides above the influence of both logic and feelings. From Its higher viewpoint better decisions can be made.

In addition to considering the impact on my home life, work, health, and finances, I looked to the inner Prophet for help in the decision-making process. The help I had asked for came to me in the form of a dream. In it I found myself in a brightly lit airport on one of the inner spiritual Heavens. I had just gotten off a plane when to my surprise, I spotted my sister seated in a waiting area up ahead. I looked forward with joyful anticipation to surprising her as I approached. Her face came alive with a beautiful smile as she stood to greet me. Our meeting was a happy one. The peace and clarity I awoke with left me with a knowingness in my heart it was okay to go. The decision turned out to be a sound one, and the trip full of blessings for each of us.

I have learned the basis for sound decisions ultimately rests on whether we have peace in our heart. A true Prophet of God has the unique ability, through dreams, contemplation, and other forms of inner communication, to show us the truth in our own heart from the viewpoint of Soul.

Written by Sandra Lane

24

A Hug Filled With God's Love

Love is the glue of the universe; it is the eternal all-creative power that holds everything together. It is God's Love for Soul that gives us life. It is our love for each other that inspires acts of kindness and sacrifice. For the serious seeker becoming more adept at giving and receiving love is a must. Fortunately most every experience we have in life can help us with this, but it is our journeys into the Heavens where we can really grow in love.

I remember it like it was yesterday. We were in class at Guidance for a Better Life and the Prophet of our times, Del Hall III, offered us the opportunity to spiritually travel as Soul to one of God's many spiritual Temples. He guided us out of our physical bodies and as Soul escorted us to the temple. I was the last to arrive, and as I did I saw everyone standing on the stairs patiently waiting.

Just then the grand doors slowly began to open. A great white light shown through; it was so intense yet I did not have to shield my eyes from it. I could feel the love and comfort flowing out through the light, it was so inviting. Then a figure appeared in the doorway, the temple guardian. A tall, thin man with a white beard dressed in a hooded white robe. I could see his eyes from a distance as they looked into me with love. He motioned to me. The Prophet and I climbed the stairs to meet him. As we approached he spoke no audible words yet I heard him welcome us. He took my hand and led me into a beautiful rotunda.

This was the most beautiful place I had ever seen. As I looked around in awe he caught my eyes and I heard, "Look up." I followed his gaze and saw the most amazing blue light emanating from the many windows that encompassed this enormous room. The blue light seemed to be alive. It had no physical source that I could see; yet it seemed to move in and around everything. Inside the temple there were no shadows, only light. The guardian in the robe again took me by the hand and looked deeply into me. His gaze was strong and full of love. He gave me a gift as the Prophet and I were getting ready to leave.

He gave me a hug, something so simple yet so amazing. It was full of everything I could ever need. I was filled with love, comfort, confidence, and the list goes on.

God knows exactly what we need and when we need it. I thanked the gentleman and the Prophet for the amazing experience, and we walked to the door. I stopped briefly to turn and look at that light one more time before we left. AMAZING! Since I arrived at Guidance for a Better Life my life has been blessed. I am so grateful to have been able to experience God's Love and Light in this truly awesome temple. Thank you Prophet for being my spiritual guide both on the inner and the outer.

Written by Anthony Allred

25

Reach Out and Bless Someone

~~~~~~~~~~~~~~~~~~~~~

We are each known and loved by God, and it is no small thing to recognize this in our daily life. Becoming aware God has read our heart and bestowed us with a personalized gift of love serves as a beautiful reminder we are never truly alone.

Often there are times in our lives we feel the need for a hug, a smile, more love, a friend — the list could be endless. At these times it is important to find a way to reach out and give a gift of love to someone else without expecting anything in return. No strings attached. This is something I have learned at Guidance for a Better Life. For example, if we are feeling the need for love in our life, instead of waiting, wishing, and hoping someone will reach out to us with love, find a way to give a gift of love to someone else. This gift of love may or may not come back directly from the one it was given to, but love will come back from somewhere. In other words, to get love, first give love!

Last spring I was reminded of this pearl of wisdom in a most unexpected way. Over the past few months I had been renting a room from a friend. The previous evening he let me know he had just been offered a new job and would need his own space during the transition period and I would need to find another place to live. Although I trusted it would all work out in the best way for everyone involved, it was weighing on my heart when I arrived at the fitness center.

As I opened my locker door I heard the radio announcer over the intercom suggest we look around and see who we could share a hug with, and how important hugs are in our lives. Well, I looked around, and the only person in my area was a little elderly lady in her eighties. She looked very tired and rather sad. I walked over and asked her if she could use a hug, adding that I sure could! We shared a hug, and she immediately brightened up. We talked for quite awhile. It was wonderful to get to know a little about this woman Frances. And I ended up sharing with her about my housing situation. This was the beginning of a beautiful friendship that God arranged!

Frances and I always enjoy the delight of interacting when we see each other at the fitness center. I have learned much more about her and her family, who live at a distance. Right before Thanksgiving I was working out in the weights section when I happened to see her going to another area of the gym. I had the inner nudge to take the time to go and visit with her. We had the most beautiful time together sharing about our Thanksgiving plans. It has been such a rich blessing to have her friendship.

That first day we met I was in need of a hug and a friend, whether I was aware of it or not. God read my heart and gave me a most beautiful gift, perfectly timed with the radio announcer talking about sharing a hug. Thanks to the teachings at Guidance for a Better Life I was open to making the first move, with prompting, to reach out to someone else. And it has blessed us both, way beyond that initial hug. Look around you and see who you can reach out to and be a blessing to today. It is a joyful and rewarding adventure of living in the present moment with the Lord.

Written by Jan Reid

26

I Finally Found Him

❡❡❡❡

Quite often it is pain and loneliness that inspire Soul to turn and reach out for God. Whatever the motivation, when a seeker is truly ready — the teacher will appear.

I grew up on a ranch near a small town in the mountains of California. It was a great place to grow up, pristine and beautiful. Hard work was the way of life, but it was good and very fulfilling. I had much to be thankful for. However, this was a logging community and drinking was the pastime during the off-season. My dad was an alcoholic, a fact that became more painfully clear as time went on. In my early twenties I was out on my own. I too was drinking heavily at the time and had just moved away from a group of friends who also drank too much. They were good people, but I needed to change the direction of my life. The problem was I was very lonely. I started going out again and drank to fill the void. I was really afraid I would turn out like my dad.

One day after a heavy night of drinking I was feeling very bad physically and filled with guilt that I had done it again. The loneliness was stronger than ever, and I began to despair. I cried out to God for help. I could not go on this way. Suddenly I felt a presence in my room. The despair and guilt in my heart lifted and was replaced by joy and happiness, more than I had ever known. My awareness of the presence did not last long, but the love that filled my heart continued to well up, bringing tears of joy. God heard my prayer and sent someone to answer it and I would never forget it. Thus began my search for answers. Who was this being who had answered my prayer to God? Could I find him again?

I now had purpose and direction in my life. I eventually gave up drinking, thanks to the Grace of God, and began my search in earnest. I read everything I could get my hands on, but there were only vague hints, just enough to keep me going. The only time I felt like I was close was when I was out in nature relaxed and at peace. It was not until later that I learned when we are peaceful and relaxed we can hear the Divine best, listening with an open heart.

I was at a bookstore one day browsing through books, even though I did not know what I was looking for. I picked up a book on wilderness survival, and to my delight, there was a school close to my home near Philadelphia, Pennsylvania. I knew I would eventually take classes, even though I put the book back. I wandered into a totally unrelated area, and to my surprise, there was the same book at eye level facing me. I laughed out loud. I knew I was being guided. I bought the book and signed up for classes. At one class I was standing alone looking around. I had really enjoyed the classes, and the location was within an hour of where I lived, but I had not found what I was looking for. I was wondering if I was going to come back. Behind me I heard a voice that sent an electric spark through me. "Spirit is actually very gentle." I turned around quickly and got my first glimpse of Del Hall III. He was talking to someone else, but I felt that one sentence had been meant for me too.

Del and I did not speak to each other at the class, but when a brochure for Guidance for a Better Life came in the mail, I signed up immediately. I knew this retreat center was for me. I was not conscious of it at the time, but I had found the Prophet of God in the physical, the being who had answered my prayer to God many years before. And so my spiritual journey began in earnest. I had found my teacher. Thank you Prophet for guiding me to you.

Written by Gary Caudle

27

Gently Awoken

Sometimes we need a little nudge to wake us from our spiritual slumber and stir us to seek the Kingdom of Heaven.

Many years ago after entering the work force under the degree I obtained, I had some adjusting to do. I was adjusting to a new job, living in a small apartment, being on my own, and having a long commute to work each day. However, I did know I was not alone and that God was with me, and with God I moved through my day.

One morning I was oversleeping. I had at the time a fifty-five minute drive to work and would have been late if I slept any longer. Of course I did not know this because I was still asleep; however God sent one of His helpers, whom I now know to be a spiritual master, to wake me. He woke me by giving me a short and quick push on my left hip, which was hard enough to wake me, yet gentle at the same time. I stirred from sleep, fumbled to see what the clock read, and saw I was indeed running late. I knew if I did not move quickly and get up I would be late for work. I was raised to be on time and to be dependable; and it was important to me to be prompt, especially with this new employment in the field I had studied in college.

I recognized I had been visited by a beautiful man with a long white robe and beard and very large eyes. This being left me with a calming love in my heart and mind as I drove to work. I sensed I was being protected and lovingly watched over; and really what more could I want? My heart soared with gratitude, love, and an excitement for living. It turns out I was beginning to wake up in another way — spiritually

I have never forgotten this gift of love, this gentle push that woke me up. It is quite significant because not many months later I was led to Guidance for a Better Life. I knew in my heart, at my first visit, this was a special place and that Del Hall III was a man of God. I was also able to make the connection that the Hand of God was giving me a push to continue my spiritual journey, and encouraging me to stay open to learn and to grow. Here with Prophet's help and guidance I have been taught the ways of God and helped to wake up as Soul. I now recognize I am valuable in the eyes of God, and I have been given an extraordinary opportunity to be helped with manifesting my Divine qualities that are gifts from God. Thank you Del for guiding and teaching me.

Written by Moira C. Cervone

28

He Hears You — Do You Hear Him?

Have you ever questioned, "Why doesn't God answer me?" after you have called out to Him in prayer. Just because you did not hear a voice coming from the Heavens does not mean He has not answered you. Most likely the answer has been staring you in the face the whole time. God speaks to us in so many different ways; we just have to know how to listen. In this testimony the author shares three different examples of how God answered his prayers. With a little bit of effort on our part we too can recognize and accept many of the blessings God is offering us.

That hot shower first thing in the morning is about as important to me as a cup of coffee is for most people to start the day. One morning as I slowly began to wake up with the shower spraying down on me, I noticed I was standing in a few inches of water. The drain could not keep up with the shower. I did not think it was a big deal because it had all drained out by the time I finished drying off. After a few weeks the water got deeper and my sacred shower had become much less enjoyable. The weekend came around and I picked up a plunger from the hardware store, hoping to quickly resolve my problem. After several hours of plunging mixed with a few minutes of cursing, I called it a day. That night as I showered before bed, it was like taking a bath and a shower at the same time. My shower was mocking me and I knew it.

With the failure of the day still fresh in my mind, I prayed for help regarding the matter and then drifted off to sleep. That night I was given a dream in which my brother-in-law came over to the house with a plunger. In the dream he showed me I needed two plungers to free up the clog in the drain. When I woke up the next morning I knew exactly what I needed to do. It wasn't five minutes after I got back from the store with an extra plunger that I had recovered a few small, foam letters from the drain that my daughter had played with during her bath. Miraculously enough, the next time I took a shower the drain worked perfectly. Prayer answered. Her foam alphabet collection was back up to twenty-six letters, and my shower was fixed. Dreams are just one of the ways God can communicate with us, but there are so many more if we know where and how to look.

Recently I did a contemplation where I asked what I could do to be a better husband to my wife and father for my children. Essentially, I prayed for help to become better in those areas. There was no booming voice that came down from the Heavens giving me the secret answers. However, after some quiet time following my prayer I had a few specific ideas that came to me. Without getting lost in the details, I had a starting point. Prayer answered. But the Divine was not finished. Later in the afternoon I heard an interview with an author on the radio. The author had written on the very points I was given during my contemplation and had even offered a few more steps beyond what I already had. I took this as acknowledgment I was on the right track. Not only was my prayer continuing to be answered, but there were even more blessings to follow. That night as my wife and I were lying in bed, she shared an article she came across on the Internet. She was not aware of my prayer during contemplation earlier in the day but had managed to find an article on exactly what I was given first thing that morning. God heard my prayer and not only answered it, but helped to keep it alive and fresh throughout the day. In retrospect I cannot help but wonder if I would have missed these gifts from God had I not learned some of the many ways the Divine can communicate with us.

I have been dealing with a personal problem for many years that has affected work, relationships, and probably my personality to some degree or another. A short time back I was literally down on my knees asking God for help. "Help me figure out how to fix this." I have probably uttered that prayer in some form before, but this time I was not asking God to fix it, I was asking for His help. The answer to that particular prayer came a few days later in the form of a flat tire. I was driving my kids to meet their stepdad so they could go back to his house. The three of us were singing Vanilla Ice's song "Ice Ice Baby," a favorite song we sing together. Somewhere between A1A and Beachfront Ave we heard a loud boom. It wasn't my speakers. It came from the pothole that jumped out and grabbed my rear tire. I knew right away the tire was gone. I was able to pull the car into a church parking lot a few hundred yards up the road. It had been a long time since I had to change a flat, and I was not excited to have to change this one on a cold and windy day. I popped the trunk, grabbing the spare tire and all of the tools I had to change it, but found I was missing the lug nut wrench. Ultimately I had to call for a wrecker to help me change the tire. Obviously the first thought I had was that this is a lesson on being prepared. However, the reason this experience is such a big deal to me is because during the forty minutes or so I waited for the service truck to arrive I was able to see a parallel between the flat tire and the personal problem I have struggled to overcome for so many years, I needed professional help. I pretty much had everything I needed to keep the car on the road; I just needed help from a professional to change the tire.

I think we all have an innate knowing that when we call out to God He actually hears us. I imagine, though, that less of us can confidently say we know He answers our prayers. These are just three examples of the different ways you might be missing your answers. God loves us beyond our comprehension, and when we make Him part of our lives it opens the door to so much love and so many blessings.

Written by Brian Boucher

29

Captain's Chair

*God created us to live our lives from the higher
dynamic viewpoint of Soul, not the lower rigid mental
state. Until our mind is on board with this arrangement
and takes a backseat to Soul, it will throw quite a fuss.
No better is the difference between mind and Soul and
the battle for top dog illustrated than in this testimony.*

Our family had just finished a delicious
evening meal and was enjoying some quality
time together in the living room. I had settled
into my chair, put my feet up to relax after a day
at work, and was enjoying watching our two-
year-old daughter play. My wife and I began to
share our day when our daughter got up from
playing, came over, and told me to get up out of
my chair.

I explained to her I was enjoying sitting in my
chair. She then got very animated and put her
hands under my legs trying her best to lift me
out of my chair and said, "Up Daddy." I firmly

told her that this was my chair, and I was not moving. She then began to cry and throw a tantrum screaming "My chair Daddy." My wife and I looked at each other with disbelief and a slight smile for this was an exceptional two-year-old moment, even for her, and not her normal behavior. I did not know why, but felt a strong urge to stay firm no matter what she did and stay sitting in my chair. I knew it was best for her. I proceeded to explain to her this was Daddy's chair, but she could sit with me if she liked. She screamed louder, and the tears were running down both sides of her now-flushed red cheeks as she stood there crying and screaming over and over, "Get up Daddy, it is my chair, get up Daddy, it is my chair. Get up Daddy, it is my chair." After about five minutes of this behavior there was no sign of letting up, so my wife took our daughter for a bath to calm her down.

This caught my attention for this was over the top behavior even for a two-year-old child. I was left with a sense of peace. I had a knowing that being firm in my attitude, that I was not going to get up no matter what, was best for all involved. Our daughter got her bath, calmed down, and we all went about our evening.

A few weeks later Prophet was helping me and a group of students understand more about our true nature as Soul. A smile came across my face as the memories of my daughter's behavior a few weeks earlier came rushing into my consciousness. I was given the clarity to see how it tied into our conversation, and it reminded me of a spiritual truth that Del has taught me over the years. Soul belongs in charge of our mind and not the other way around. Soul belongs in the captain's chair of our life. We are Soul, the spiritual adult in the relationship with the mind. It is much like the loving relationship between a parent and a child.

The mind, we call the "little-self," is much like a two-year-old and was never designed to run our life. The mind is very limited and is the source of our frustrations, fears, anger, worries, self-doubts, vanity, attachments, and a variety of other ailments. It does not like change, gets overwhelmed, and is generally closed to ideas outside of itself. These are all traits of the mind but not of Soul. The mind is good at balancing our checkbooks and taking care of our daily tasks, but it is very limited when compared to the boundlessness of Soul.

Soul is creative, resilient, happy, peaceful, and cherishes freedom. It also has clarity, a can-do attitude, access to wisdom, and is generally open to new ideas. Soul has a higher spiritual consciousness than the mind, thus better equipped to run our lives. Soul is free to travel the Heavens, has a greater capacity to give and receive love, and Its potential for growth has no limits.

When we begin to be more spiritually nourished, Soul grows stronger in our life. We begin to make better choices and decisions that benefit us and those we love. Some of the things that help Soul grow stronger are singing HU, reading scriptures, paying attention to dreams, spending time with Prophet, and learning to recognize and be grateful for the blessings in life.

When Soul begins to get stronger the mind may start to protest. At first it feels threatened and does not want to give up sitting in the captain's chair. The little-self has been used to being in charge of our life and has grown to like telling us how things should be. Initially the mind does not like the idea of Soul being in charge and will protest, yell, and scream, much like a two-year-old throwing tantrums to get its way. When Soul gains enough strength it takes charge of the mind and takes its rightful place in the captain's chair of our life. This is what is best for us and what is best for our little-self.

Our true self, Soul, is designed by God to be in charge of the mind. Soul has a higher view of life, sees more clearly, and is receptive to God's Love, truth, and guidance. As Soul we are more relaxed, peaceful, joyous, loving, wise, and creative. God actually created the mind to be subservient to Soul; an instrument to be used by Soul to achieve its purpose during its sojourn on planet Earth. This experience is a reminder to me that I want to live my life with Soul in charge of the little-self. That I want to nourish Soul daily and feed it the spiritual food it needs to grow stronger and stay strong, because this is my Divine nature — Soul. It is the true expression of myself as God created me.

Thank you Prophet for giving me this experience and for helping me manifest my Divine nature and the dreams of my heart.

Written by Mark Snodgrass

30

God Guided My Doctor

One of many ways the Holy Spirit can "speak" to us is through what many commonly refer to as a "gut feeling." That inner knowingness we are on track and making the right decision. It not only blesses us but also those we come in contact with in our lives if we learn to recognize, trust, and follow this Divine guidance. In the following story it quite literally saves someone's life.

At a medical appointment in April of 2016 it came as a surprise to me when my doctor suggested I have surgery, a hysterectomy. I had been experiencing some abnormal symptoms for about six months. He made several adjustments to my hormone treatments over that time, but the symptoms would not go away. In prayer and contemplation I asked Prophet for guidance and help in deciding whether this surgery was in my best interest physically and spiritually. Prophet is the current manifestation of God's Holy Spirit. He is the Voice of God, the Comforter of our time, the Hand of God. Prophet Del Hall III teaches and guides us in the outer physical world and in the inner spiritual worlds. I know Prophet is always with me spiritually. I am so grateful for his presence in my life. He gave me a sense of peace about the surgery and a knowing it was the right thing to do.

This type of surgery is fairly routine, and I felt confident in my doctor's ability and experience since he has performed it many times. He told me I would not need to have the surgery immediately; I could enjoy my summer and have it done in the fall. I knew I could trust what he said because when I was searching for a new doctor about two years before, I prayed for help and guidance. I know Prophet led me to this particular doctor. I would soon find out what a life-saving gift this was!

The surgery took place in late September. Walking up the sidewalk to the hospital with my husband Paul in the early hours of that Tuesday morning, we sang HU together, a pure prayer and love song to God. I felt blessed and very much at peace knowing the inner Prophet was with Paul and me then, and would be with us throughout the surgery. I prayed Prophet would guide my doctor and his medical team. While I was in the prep area before surgery I was again silently singing HU. My doctor visited me and talked with me, calming the slight jitters I had started to feel. Prophet was showing me his love and comfort through the doctor's words. I told my doctor God had led me to him. Although he did not respond verbally, his eyes and smile expressed his recognition of this truth.

Later that day after the surgery, the doctor stopped by my hospital room to check on how I was recovering. He shared that the surgery turned out to be much more than a routine hysterectomy. He had discovered a large mass surrounding my bladder. He faced the challenge of carefully cutting and peeling away the mass without seriously damaging the bladder. He was happy to share he successfully accomplished this in addition to the hysterectomy. I am so grateful to Prophet and to my doctor for this amazing blessing! At that time in the hospital room, neither the doctor nor I was aware of an even greater blessing that resulted from the surgery.

At the follow-up appointment one week later my doctor had more amazing news to share with Paul and me. He looked and sounded very touched emotionally as he spoke. He had received a phone call from the pathology lab two days prior and was told that a cancerous tumor had been found in one of the ovaries he removed. He had considered not removing my ovaries, however, at some point prior to the day of surgery he changed his mind. He said he had a gut feeling to remove them, and trusts his gut feelings because they are always right. I felt an inner nudge from Prophet to share with my doctor that his gut feelings are Divine guidance from God, and it is so awesome he trusts them! My doctor agreed. He looked into my eyes and said, "You are a very blessed woman."

If he had not followed Prophet's guidance — his gut feeling — and had decided to leave the ovaries in place, the cancer could have spread and perhaps not been found for a long time or at all. This could have resulted in complicated physical problems, radiation and chemo treatments, and quite possibly my physical death for this lifetime. As it was the ovaries were carefully removed intact. The pathologist assured my doctor that he did not need to refer me to an oncologist; the cancer had been removed completely.

My doctor did not know about the mass on the bladder nor the cancer before the surgery. He shared that several times during the surgery he paused, pushed his chair back from the robotic surgical console, and took a deep breath before deciding what steps to take next. Prophet was guiding him throughout the surgery. He was receiving Prophet's help and guidance by way of his gut feelings — while I was on the operating table!

My doctor said if he had tried to remove the ovaries through the small abdominal incisions he had made the cancer could have spread internally. Also, had he tried to perform the hysterectomy in the conventional way without laparoscopic robotic assistance, my bladder would have been seriously damaged, resulting in major complications. He followed his gut feelings to perform both procedures differently than he originally planned.

At the end of the appointment as my doctor was leaving the room, Paul and I expressed our deep appreciation to him for all he did. He said, "It wasn't me. It was God." I felt another inner nudge from Prophet to share with him that he had been an instrument for God and followed His Divine guidance to do what needed to be done.

One of the ways Prophet personally guides and communicates with us, God's children, is through gut feelings, also called inner nudges, a sixth sense, that small voice, a knowingness, or intuition. Sometimes they are gentle whisperings, sometimes very strong feelings. These are gifts of Divine love. I am grateful to be growing in my awareness of Prophet's presence, love, and the guidance he gives me through this inner communication. Prophet has given me a knowingness I would have died from the cancer within about three years. Thankfully I have fully recovered and regained my strength.

I am so blessed and extremely grateful to God's Prophet for the many blessings he has given me through this experience, and for leading me to a doctor who believes in God and is receptive to His guidance; who trusts and follows his gut feelings! Through his love, grace, and mercy, Prophet protected me from severe physical complications and suffering by guiding my doctor to perform the surgical procedures in ways that literally saved my life. Thank you Prophet for your amazing love! I love you.

Written by Cathy Sandman

31

God's Personal Response

When we reach out and draw closer to God, God does
respond. It is up to us to recognize His response, which
can manifest in infinite ways from the dramatic to the
very subtle. God can use anything to express His Love
to us. Having a grateful open heart gives us the
eyes to better see and accept this Love.

One of my favorite things to do is find a quiet
place, put aside the affairs of the day, and spend
sacred, quality time with God. Recently I was
visiting family for the Christmas holidays. I was
out on my daily run, and as I neared the end I
stopped by a marina and found a serene spot by
the water where I could sit for awhile. The
weather was chilly but still nice enough to be
outside, for which I was grateful.

Just being able to sit and experience the
beauty of God's creation had already opened my
heart, but there was so much more. As I sat
down I began to list all my blessings and my

heart swelled with gratitude: quality time spent with family over the holidays, my dear friends whom I was able to visit on my way here, a new house to move into when I got home, my teaching job, downtime, and this relaxing moment.

I humbly asked Prophet, my spiritual guide, if he would join me in singing HU, a love song to my creator. His inner spiritual presence was palpable and filled my consciousness. I reached out to him and he took my hands, clasping them firmly. I felt the warmth of his love radiate into me and I returned mine to him. My heart opened even wider with gratitude for this moment and opportunity. I now began to sing HU aloud, solely intent on giving as much love as I could in that moment. In an instant Prophet and I were at a beautiful ocean together, an ocean full of love and mercy, after singing HU and sending love to God. I remember feeling "my cup runneth over." What could possibly top this? How could this moment be any sweeter?

And then, with only the perfect timing the Divine can orchestrate, a sudden and isolated gust of wind came seemingly out of nowhere and touched my face, just as I was sending my love to God. To me it felt like an immediate response. It was an otherwise still day; I had not noticed a breath of wind since sitting down. As I purely expressed the love that was in my heart for God, He answered me. The answer came in a breath of wind, caressing my face; perhaps the way a parent might touch their child's face with affection.

To some this might appear to be just a random gust of wind, but my heart knows better. God responded to the love I sent, and this was a gift that touched me to my core. As the well-known Bible quote says, "Draw nigh to God, and he will draw nigh to you." James 4:8, KJV Wow — how amazing to know I can have experiences like those spoken of in scripture!

God can use anything to reach out and communicate with His children. In my case it was wind on an otherwise calm day. For someone else it might be the sun suddenly bursting through an overcast sky. It could be a license plate, a song on the radio, words spoken by someone with a message tailor-made for you, or in a calm inner knowingness. His ways are infinite.

Reach out to God. Express your genuine desire to know Him and experience His Love. And then listen quietly for the answer.
Written by Laurence Elder

32

Through the Eyes of Soul

Whether physically young or old, we are all first and
foremost Soul — eternal spiritual beings. We are all
children of God. When Soul tunes in spiritually it has
a higher view regardless of the physical age
of the body Soul resides in.

The room was filled with more than just
physical bodies seated in chairs, but Souls that
love God. Looking down the rows everyone
seemed appreciative to be in Prophet's presence.
The annual clean-up weekend preparing
Guidance for a Better Life retreat center grounds
for a new year was just wrapping up. We
gathered together as Del was about to lead us in
singing HU. I always enjoy this opportunity as the
group expresses to God the love and gratitude
in our hearts.

As I sat down I looked around at the beautiful
scene in that room and over at my family with a
smile on my face expressing the joy and

gratefulness in my heart. I reflected on the gift of being there together. My husband and I attend retreats offered by Prophet Del Hall III on a regular basis. This is where we learned about HU, which is also an ancient name for God. In turn we taught it to our three children and sing it at home, but on this day we would all be participating in singing together at the retreat center.

Prophet led the HU song, and our voices followed in unison, sending love to God, wave after wave as individuals and as a group. There was an immediate response from God. His beautiful Light and Love filled the room and flowed beyond. It showered down to all in attendance and created a brightness spanning throughout the space. I could feel the sound reverberating in my heart and being. This living Light and Sound of God, His Voice, seemed to draw out and showcase Divine qualities as I overflowed with joy, gratitude, and love. This beautiful cycle of giving God love and appreciation, and then receiving His Love continued with no perception of time, until Prophet ended by saying, "Thank you."

As the group dispersed I stood outside by the edge of the building holding my three-year-old son. He kept poking his finger at a post in front of us. His face looked puzzled as he continued this direct and deliberate movement. When I asked what he was doing he said, "What is that Mom?" Chuckling and slightly confused by his reaction I said, "It is wood. It is part of the building." Still displaying a perplexed look he said, "Hmm...wood, yeah. But this isn't a building, it is a light castle." I was taken aback. Everything stood still in that moment. I was amazed my son could see what I knew to be true based on my own experiences and those shared by others over the years at the retreat center.

In that moment we were both seeing through Soul's eyes, not our physical ones. We had just sung HU with open hearts in the presence of God's Prophet tuning in to Spirit, and there was a higher view before us. We were raised up to see it. My son saw clearly. He was seeing truth. He was experiencing that building as what it really is — not an illusion, but God's Light. And it is everywhere. We just need to look through a new lens. At the same time I was seeing him as Soul, maybe for the first time. It was more personal than seeing others as Soul. This was my own child, and it made an impression. Just as quickly he was back to acting like a little boy and talking about other things, but in that window of a moment my view changed.

He is my son, but really he is Soul first. I knew that, but I experienced it and that changed something. My view, perception, and interactions were different. This experience brought out a desire in me to be more aware of illustrating for my children how I am led by Prophet and love God. They are each a child of God I am blessed to care for in this life. I am privileged to guide, nurture, encourage, and help them find their way. It is not simply my job to "take care of them" in providing food, clothing, shelter, and supervision, but I am entrusted to love and guide them. I am their mother, but first and foremost they are each a child of God on loan to me to raise. Regardless of their age, they are Soul first. These messages sank into me so much deeper that day.

That one small interaction held layers of lasting truth and lessons I still think about today. With that new image of my son, I recognized my goal to be clear and focused so I may be the best teacher I can for my children. I want to model for them to the best of my ability, and I can when I am led by Spirit. We simply need to accept the Divine help and guidance that is always available to Soul; just like my little one did that morning, seeing our real surroundings through the eyes of Soul. God's Love is everywhere. Prophet wants to show those willing and ready.

Written by Michelle Hibshman

33

Multiple Healings

A healing from God may reveal itself instantaneously and the ailment is just gone, but often it takes time for a healing we received spiritually to manifest in the physical. This may come in the form of being guided to the right doctor, or even by being kept alive long enough physically until the technology catches up with our condition. Whatever the timing may be, healing is a gift of love from God through His Prophet.

Every good sailor knows if you sail on the seas of life long enough you will hit a storm. I had one roll in this past year. And though I felt the disruptive surface waves in my daily life, deep inside there remained a beautiful and calm sense of peace because Prophet was with me!

I am currently fifty-five years old. About two years ago I started having pain in my chest and shortness of breath. I had trouble breathing, falling asleep, and sleeping through the night. There were days when I was sluggish and it felt as if I was walking through mud. I went to the emergency room where they did many tests. Though the doctors determined I had not had a heart attack or stroke, to be on the safe side I was sent to a cardiologist. Over the next year I saw a number of specialists and had blood tests, allergy tests, stress tests, EKGs, CAT scans, and chest x-rays. After about ten months I was finally diagnosed with a condition called atrial fibrillation. Another test determined I also had sleep apnea which was possibly creating additional stress and exacerbating the heart arrhythmia. At the suggestion of the cardiologists I was put on blood thinners and heart medication. I also began using a CPAP machine to help me breathe more regularly as I slept. After four months there was very little improvement with the apnea so I was referred to an ear, nose, and throat doctor or ENT for short. In August of 2016 I underwent sinus and throat surgery to help remove some blockages in my airways.

During this time the heart and breathing issues continued. Some nights they became so severe I was not sure if I would be waking up in the morning. In order to get through the more challenging days I surrendered to God, more fully than I ever have before, and relied more completely on the inner Prophet than I ever thought was possible. Though the physical symptoms were hampering my daily activities in significant ways, the challenges I was facing were helping me draw closer to God. It is for this reason I look at this time as an incredible blessing, one I am extremely grateful for.

When I was in my teens my father suddenly and unexpectedly passed away. He was only forty-two years old. Though the actual cause of death was never officially determined by autopsy, it has been suggested that heart issues were the cause. In 1985 when I was twenty-four years old I had what the doctors called a lone episode of atrial fibrillation which put me in the cardiac care wing of the hospital for three days before it subsided. I had another episode about ten years later in 1995 and then a third in 2006 where I ended up back in the emergency room.

In 2015 my heart went into atrial fibrillation again, but this time it did not go away after a day or two as it had done in the past. Prophet can work out the timing and the details in our lives in such a way everything works together to benefit us in the most amazing ways. When you're under the wing of a Prophet of God everything is taken care of at the perfect time. It is my strong sense

God literally extended my physical life until modern technology was developed to more effectively address this health issue.

In 2016, along with the challenges I was having with my health, the second wave of the storm rolled in. In April my mother became ill and passed away within a relatively short period of time. We had been very close. In May a good friend passed, on July third our close neighbor did as well. A few months before his death, his wife and also a dear friend were diagnosed with stage four lung cancer. And on July fifth, due to an unexpected illness, we had to put our loved and very devoted German Shepherd to sleep.

During this time everything around me seemed so fragile: my family, friends, and even my own health. Life was showing me something I was taught by Del Hall III years ago; everything on the physical plane is on loan, nothing here is permanent or stable except our relationship with the Divine. At the same time that all these ties were being cut within the temporal world, I was leaning on and strengthening my relationship with God and His Prophet. There were days between the health issues and close personal losses that I was pushed beyond the limit of what I could bear or handle myself. The thing that kept me going every day was my relationship with the Divine! It also became very clear that on certain days Prophet often carried me through this challenging time.

In looking back on it, I feel Prophet was very aware of what 2015 and 2016 would bring into my life and knew ahead of time I would need to develop a closer relationship with him, as the inner Prophet, to help me make it through the year. In those two years I was on my knees, prayed a lot, focused daily on God's Love and guidance, and made it a point to frequently count the blessings in my life. I learned to treasure each breath, each heartbeat, and each moment with family and friends. I felt directed to specific doctors at specific times. I learned a lot about patience and trusting in God's timing, His Love, and the relationship I was developing with His Prophet. Each day when I woke up I felt blessed to be alive, and our relationship grew closer and closer and dearer to me. I know God loves me and I am never alone. As Soul I am immortal, and if I die tomorrow the love and relationship we have would continue on in the Heavenly Worlds.

After the sinus and throat surgery there were times when I was still having significant problems breathing, so in August I was sent to a pulmonologist to see if the difficulties were related to my lungs. Upon a first examination the doctor noticed an apparent problem so she scheduled me for a few more tests in the middle of September to further assess my respiratory and pulmonary systems. Prior to the second appointment with the pulmonologist I attended the "Spiritual Growth and Conditioning" retreat at Guidance for a Better Life. It was during this retreat I was blessed with the following experience and healing.

During a HU sing, on the inner as Soul, I was escorted by Prophet to the twelfth Heaven, the Ocean of Love and Mercy, and was brought before God Himself. Prophet and I were on the beach at the water's edge bowed before God. I felt a deep peace, reverence, and gratitude beyond what I had ever known before. God said to me, "Please rise my child and step forward," which I did. I stepped off the beach and out onto the Ocean of Love and Mercy where I found myself suspended slightly above the water's surface. The Ocean rose up and the Light and Sound of God flowed up into me. I was gently laid back and felt more fully surrendered to God's will and Love. Then I was filled with a deeper love and trust than I can express in words. I experienced the inner Prophet as my intercessor standing before me, next to me, and with me. He reached in and took out my heart and lungs which were made of beautiful white light. Before God he held them in his outstretched hands as if in a personal prayer to our Heavenly Father. He handed them to God, who gently and lovingly took them, held them in His Hands, and kissed them. My heart and lungs took on a golden glow more beautiful than anything of this world. Our Heavenly Father then handed them back to Prophet who lovingly placed them back into my chest. The moment Prophet put them back in my chest I gasped, taking in a deep and involuntary breath. I felt as if I was being reborn again. I found myself back on the beach and fell to my knees weeping, overwhelmed with gratitude and love.

I knew I had had a significant healing from God. Also I was given the awareness this healing would take time to filter down and manifest fully in the physical. Though for the week after the retreat I thought perhaps the healing had already manifested physically, as I had no sign of atrial fibrillation. But the following week on the morning of September 12 I woke up with the familiar chest pain and irregular heart rhythm. When I look back, the timing that the chest pain and breathing difficulty returned was perfect. I had an echocardiogram scheduled for that very afternoon. Being in atrial fibrillation at the same time the EKG was being done gave the doctors the opportunity to more clearly see and record what my heart had been doing.

As scheduled by the pulmonologist prior to the retreat, the following Thursday morning I went to have the test done to assess my lungs and breathing. Later that same afternoon I went to the doctor for the results. Even before I walked into the office I had the feeling the test was going to confirm the healing I had at the Ocean of Love and Mercy before God. When the doctor came in to speak with me she said that even though she originally thought there may have been a problem, there definitely were no signs of one now. In fact the tests showed my lungs were not only functioning normally but well beyond the favored result. Half joking she said, "We never see people in my office with a score that high. I can promise you it's definitely not your lungs!" In my heart I knew the only explanation for a result this dramatic was intervention by God.

Now that it was confirmed the pain in my chest was not caused by a problem with my lungs, and we had done what we could with my sinus issues, in late October after exhausting all other options I consented to a heart procedure called an ablation. During an ablation, catheters which are long flexible tubes, are inserted through the veins in the upper thighs. The catheters are then robotically maneuvered up to the heart. Within one of the catheters is a camera-like device and in the other are tools to map and cauterize, or burn, the area that the abnormal impulse is originating from, which in my case were the four veins that enter into the atria, or top chamber, of my heart. The scar tissue that forms creates a barrier which serves as a gasket-like buffer between the four veins and my heart. It stops the abnormal impulses from affecting the normal rhythm.

On Thursday October 27 I went for a CAT scan. The morning had been hectic and a little stressful, and I started to feel somewhat anxious. As I sat quietly refocusing on my relationship with Prophet, I experienced his presence. In Prophet's presence I was deeply comforted and felt his peace, love, and the reassurance everything would be fine. He also reminded me I had already experienced the healing from God at the Ocean of Love and Mercy and that it would continue to manifest into the physical world. Then as I sat waiting for the technician to come into the room, I literally saw the vacant physician's chair next to me roll a few inches across the floor. As you can imagine this caused my eyebrows to rise, but I knew Prophet was showing me he was truly right there next to me. This brought peace, comfort, and an even greater confirmation and reassurance that no matter what happened I was not alone.

Friday October 28, Ablation Day. From the time I woke up in the morning through every moment and everything that occurred during the rest of the day, I could feel God's Love and His Prophet's presence with me. I was also aware of the love and prayers that were being sent by family and friends. Prayers are real and can definitely have a positive impact on the outcome of a situation. The hospital staff prepped me; I kissed my wife goodbye, and was wheeled to the operating room. Prophet never left my side. And though I know he is always with me, I'm not always consciously aware of it so I was doubly grateful. Not only was he with me, but I was allowed to perceive his presence so clearly and for such an extended period of time. Once we arrived I was allowed to walk into the ablation room. It looked like a NASA control center. There were about fifteen large monitors and a large glass window behind which were another technician and control room to be used during the procedure. I do not think I fully realized the gravity and seriousness of the procedure until that moment. I was now more acutely aware of the risks and how skilled and precise the surgeon needed to be to successfully perform the ablation. I was also aware that a small slip or error in judgment could change my life or even end it. Yet a feeling of deep peace remained with me. As I lay down on the table I felt Prophet standing beside me holding my hand. I literally felt him squeeze my hand and move it a few inches from where it lay, which helped to reinforce that he was there. I just smiled as I drifted off to sleep under the anesthetic.

The next thing I remembered was a very bright light above me, then I left my body and was floating with Prophet about six feet above the table. For a while we watched the operation as the doctors and technicians did their job, and then I was escorted into the Light of God. That was all I recalled until I woke up in the recovery room. The doctor said everything had gone smoothly, and the procedure appeared to have resolved the issue. A day later I was back home with instructions to rest for a few more days. Since the operation I have not experienced any more episodes of atrial fibrillation.

Instead of an immediate healing by a miraculous wave of His Hand, God will sometimes use or work through a specific doctor or practitioner to bring His healing into our lives, which certainly is no less miraculous though sometimes this is not as apparent. In my case I felt strongly that one of the amazing ways God blessed me was through the cardiologist who performed the ablation procedure. In November I had a follow-up sleep test to check how successful the surgeries had been. The results were great. I had no sign of sleep apnea; there were no blockages, and no sign of atrial fibrillation. My sleeping blood pressure, heart rate, and oxygen levels were all very good. The sleep specialist said the ENT and ablation surgeries seemed to have gone remarkably well and it looked like they had fixed everything.

I know all three physical healings I was graced with this year, on my heart, lungs, and sinuses, were latter manifestations of those I first received from God at the Ocean of Love and Mercy. I also have a sense the healings went much deeper than simply physical problems. I feel they also addressed and affected deeply rooted karmic issues I have possibly carried for thousands of years from lives I have lived in the past. My sense is that without Prophet's intervention and God's healing my life span would have been much shorter than it now has the potential to be. Only God and His Prophet can alter which day we are possibly scheduled to translate. Only they can go to the root cause and heal us from our past-life karma.

Prophet is my intercessor and advocate. Because I had never before experienced a more powerful example of what an intercessor is as I have this year, I felt drawn to look up and research the definition of the word. Intercede means "to interpose on behalf of one in difficulty or in trouble…" In the gospel an intercessor is a go-between or advocate who represents and pleads our case to God. Prophet is my comforter: One who sat with me in my times of need bringing me peace, love, comfort, and reassurance. He is my healer: Through Prophet, God healed me of my current health issues, and some long-buried karma of the past. He is my guide: One who repeatedly helped me find my way to the best care at the most optimal time. More importantly Prophet continues to show me the most appropriate, beneficial, and helpful steps to take in an ever-growing relationship with the Divine. He is my friend: One who never left me and never will. An agent of change: One who miraculously and in the most beneficial ways forever changed the course of my life, both spiritually and physically. Prophet is the Light of God, the Wayshower and the Way: One who brings the Light of God into my life and brings me into the Light of God, and continues to lead me on the way back home to God.

Dear Prophet, I thank you with every breath and with all my heart! Thank you for your love, blessings, and healings. I know this all came about because of your love and my relationship with you, God's chosen Prophet. Thank you!

Written by Jason Levinson

34

More Love for My Cat Buster

It is a joy and sacred privilege when we have the opportunity to be a point of light in this world and pass on God's Love to those around us. It matters not if it's a friend, family member, neighbor, or in the following case — a beloved pet.

On a recent Saturday evening I sat happily tired in my favorite chair. I looked back on a satisfying and productive day spent working outside. I had made good progress towards completion of a new doghouse and kennel addition. I love to build things, and building for my pets is especially sweet. I had asked Prophet to join me in all I did that day. His inner presence brought insights and nudges on ways to make things snug, comfortable, and secure for our dogs. And maybe to the dogs' disappointment, also better at keeping our tasty free-range chickens out of the dog kennel. Our two older dogs and ten-month-old newly adopted puppy kept me company. The puppy found places to hide my things, especially my leather work gloves. His antics opened my heart more and more as the day progressed. My wife Diane was away for the weekend, and I had promised to take good care of our two gray and white cats, Buster and Charlie. More important than feeding them and cleaning the litter box was to "love them up," as we call it.

So as I sat in my chair Buster appeared almost as soon as I elevated the footrest and placed a blanket over my legs. He jumped up into one of his favorite spots, stretching out on the footrest between my knees and feet. With us situated this way I could just reach his lower back. Buster purred loudly as I extended my hand and began to pet him. A prayer formed in my heart for Buster to really feel loved. I soon felt an inner nudge to simply lay both my open hands on his back, palms down, without moving them. Buster continued to purr as I felt my hands grow warmer. To my surprise, I felt and saw another pair of hands lovingly overlay my own hands, and then merge with them.

Prophet has blessed me many times over the years with his love and touch, so I was excited and grateful when I instantly recognized these were his hands. Prophet's hands brought more of God's gentle, golden Love to pass on to Buster, an answer to my prayer. As God's Love passed through our hands to Buster I was blessed to be part of that special moment. This was the surprise highlight of an all-around great day filled with God's blessings, infinitely better than icing on a cake.

Several days later as I sat and wrote of the above moment when our hands were on Buster's back, he actually jumped up on the table in front of me and interrupted my writing. As if to add an exclamation point that he had indeed felt God's Love, and that my prayer for him had indeed been answered, Buster purred loudly and rubbed insistently against my chin until he was sure I got his message.

Like our other pets Buster is a gift from God that opens our hearts to love. He is a gift to help us learn to give and receive more love in this lifetime, a vital and joyful way to grow spiritually. I am happiest when there is a balance between giving and receiving love. The more love I accept the more I can pass on. And conversely the more love I pass on the more love God sends me to accept. This is a wonderful way to live, neither the beginning nor the end point but within the flow of God's Love. This brings a deep sense of joy and fulfillment for me as Soul, my true eternal self. Buster is one of the countless blessings in the abundant life I live because of God's Grace. I am grateful God's Prophet teaches me to see and appreciate so many blessings. I would not hold them so dear in my heart without his help.

Written by Irv Kempf

35

God Blessed Us a Vacation

❦

Life should include work and play — we need both. To have all of one or the other would put us out of balance. Fortunately God knows this better than most and will help us to walk this line.

My husband and I are in the middle of a massive house renovation, replacing all our siding and fixing a lot of water damage. We are blessed to be able to do most the work ourselves and save quite a bit of money. We have been working hard all summer, my husband especially; every free minute he does something to move the project along another step. Things are really starting to come together! We had been talking about taking a vacation, just a quick weekend trip away from all the construction. As the time passed we kept talking about it but had nothing planned. It was in our hearts to have some relaxing time away.

My husband had been searching online for a trip to surprise me with; he was looking for a nice weekend away together. He was also praying to God and Prophet for help to guide us to the perfect weekend retreat, but not yet found anything online that seemed like the right trip. Then, "out of the blue," a friend of mine sent me a message asking if we wanted to join them on their vacation the following weekend. He had planned a surprise weekend away in Hatteras, North Carolina for his wife. He said, "I know it is short notice, far away, and you probably can't come, but I woke up this morning and thought how fun would it be if you came with us!" God was speaking to him. He even offered to pay for our room!

Although we did not feel right letting him pay for the entire trip, we did appreciate his gift of love to us and allowed him to pay for some of our room. We've learned from Prophet we are here on Earth to learn how to give and receive love. We felt if we completely denied his offer we would also be denying his chance to pass on this love gift. It is equally important to learn to receive love, and this was a beautiful example.

When he offered for us to join them I immediately knew this was a gift from God! We recognized how God lined up all the little details to give us this vacation. We were actually free that weekend, when normally we are pretty busy on weekends, but miraculously we were not scheduled for anything. Also it worked out that my husband, who does not have a lot of vacation time, had to work one evening during the week, so he could take Friday off without using a vacation day! The vacation was exactly what we needed — a few days away from the construction at a beautiful inn on the Pamlico Sound.

We really enjoyed our time together and our time with some great friends. This was an answer to our prayers; God heard my husband's prayer and God read my heart! Even though I did not verbalize my prayer, God knew the prayer in my heart. God and Prophet gifted us with the perfect weekend retreat for which we are very grateful!

Written by Emily Allred

36

Spared by a Hair

Keep your heart and mind open to the little things in life that seem to slow you up or change your plans in one way or another. Instead of becoming frustrated and letting them close your heart, consider perhaps they may be a blessing of protection, and be grateful.

One morning as I was going about my normal routine getting ready for work my hair dryer stopped working. It had on rare occasions in the past done the same thing, but it did not happen very often. Usually I would not have time to wait for it to start working again, so I would just skip that step in my routine and continue on. On this particular day I heard the voice of the inner Prophet say very clearly that this was meant to delay me by a few minutes. I had the conscious thought; "This is one of those times that a two-minute delay saves you from getting into a car accident." I trusted completely this was the case whether I ever received outer confirmation or not.

I had been softly aware of Prophet's presence throughout the morning, but after my hair dryer stopped working and I heard his inner voice, I slowed down and very deliberately asked Prophet to come with me to work that day. It was a good reminder that consciously asking to be in Prophet's presence is better than just knowing he is always with me. I stood in my bathroom and hit the test and reset buttons on my hair dryer for about a minute. My husband came into the bathroom, and I told him my hair dryer had stopped working, but I was not going to get frustrated or rush because I knew it was Divine protection. On that particular day I was leaving early to pick up my sister who had asked for a ride to work. The extra stop meant I really needed to stay on schedule to make sure I made it to work on time, but the Divine communication overrode everything I was "supposed to do."

After a minute or two the hair dryer resumed working and I completed my routine. I picked up my sister a few minutes late and we headed down the highway to the neighboring town where we both work. About fifteen minutes into the drive I noticed traffic was slowing down and starting to merge into the right lane. Up ahead was a multi-car accident. Fortunately it did not look like anyone was seriously hurt, but it was definitely not the way they had intended to start their day. There were three cars that had rear-ended one another and then a few yards back another four cars in their own wreck, most likely as a result of the first wreck.

The accident had literally happened just a few minutes before we came upon it. There were no emergency vehicles on-site yet. One woman was sitting in her car dialing her phone. One man was gingerly climbing out of his car and looking back at the scene. Another woman was holding her face and slowly shaking her head, as her air bag had deployed. The car engines were still smoking. I looked at my sister and told her what had happened while I was getting ready for work. We both knew without a doubt we were protected by Prophet.

When I arrived home that evening I shared with my husband what had transpired. He said he had prayed for extra Divine protection for me that morning as I drove away. He had heard me say I felt my hair dryer was slowing me down on purpose and wanted to pray for protection.

Later that evening I shared the story with my father, Del Hall III, God's Prophet of the times. We live on the same property, and he shared with me he had consciously given me a double-dose of protection that morning when I drove by on my way to work. When he hears a family member drive by on the way to town he often places a bubble of God's Light, as Divine protection, around them and their vehicle. On that particular day he had felt drawn to make it a double-dose. He had not known consciously that my sister was going to be riding in the car with me, but it partially explains the double-dose of protection he bestowed upon his two daughters.

If I had not seen the car accident as outer confirmation I still trusted I was being delayed for some Divine reason. God's timing and God's plan are always at work. I am grateful for the eyes to see and the heart to know.

Written by Catherine Hughes

37

To Do or To Be?

Every hour of every day is another opportunity to be led by Spirit and grow closer to God. Especially when following through with a sacred prayer that has been shared by Prophet.

I was preparing for bed on the first night of a retreat at Guidance for a Better Life. The air was cool and crisp, yet I felt the warmth of God's Love all around me as I took a deep, cleansing breath and let it out slowly. Our teacher, Prophet Del Hall III, had given us a "Three-Part Prayer" that can be done at bedtime, or at any other time, to strengthen one's relationship with God. The first part is to think of something I am grateful for from that day. This helps me recognize daily blessings from God delivered through His Prophet. Second, to ask Prophet for a dream or any experience that will help build my relationship with him. Third, to let Prophet know I will be receptive to what is given. That night, before going to sleep, there was no way I could have imagined how amazing God's response would be.

Lying in my sleeping bag, I thought of how grateful I was to be there as a student of God's chosen Prophet of the times, who has the ability to teach us in the outer physical realm and also in the inner spiritual realm as the inner Prophet, God's Holy Spirit. This gratitude opened my heart. My next thought was how grateful I was to be warm and snug in my sleeping bag on the soft bed of fresh straw. This further opened my heart, helping me be more receptive to God's Love in whatever form it came. I prayed, asking Prophet for a dream or an experience that would help build my relationship with him. Then I let him know I was receptive to whatever he gave. Prophet had said God's response to the "Three-Part Prayer" may come in a dream or later in an awake experience. It came in both of these ways!

My dream journal was beside me, and I had a pen and flashlight ready. I began to silently sing HU as I drifted off to sleep. That night I was given a dream. In the dream I was looking at my to-do list in front of me. There were twenty-four items on the list. I turned away from the list and looked toward Prophet, who was standing beside me. As I turned to him the items on the list came alive and expanded up and off the page. That is when I woke up.

It was the middle of the night. I immediately rolled over and wrote the dream in my journal because I knew if I went right back to sleep I might not remember the dream when I woke up again. I prayed, asking Prophet for clarity on what the dream meant and then went back to sleep. I awoke some time later with more clarity about the dream. Prophet revealed to me that by turning away from my to-do list and looking toward him, the items on the list were immediately transformed and upgraded from tasks I was to do to opportunities to be with Prophet, the Holy Spirit, and have help in doing each task. I was excited and grateful for the gift of this Divine insight. It was still very early in the morning, so I lay there in Prophet's loving inner presence. I realized how awesome life could be if I actually integrated this insight into my life. Eventually I fell asleep again.

When I awoke the third time another piece of the puzzle was given to me. Why were there twenty-four items on the list in my dream? I asked Prophet whether this could represent a twenty-four-hour day. Yes! By turning to him in everything I do, my days and nights are no longer just filled with things to do, including sleep, they are filled with opportunities to be with him and have his Divine help. Wow!

I knew this could help build my relationship with God through His Prophet, and I knew it could help me live a better life. I am accustomed to asking for God's help through His Prophet with the big things in life. Now in response to this dream I want to grow into remaining aware his help is always available for the asking, even with all the seemingly small things in life.

The next day of the retreat was filled with Prophet's loving guidance and teaching that stirred within me a deeper love and appreciation for my teacher Del and a strong desire to be a better student of God's teachings. By the end of the day I was eager to integrate more of what I had learned into my life. On the ride home I was excited and joyful because Prophet had given me clarity about life changes I can make.

The morning after returning home from the retreat I got up early and sat quietly with Prophet, asking him how best to use this time. He nudged me to look at my to-do list for the day. I was thinking there was no way I could get all this done today. Then I remembered the dream. I closed my eyes and knowing Prophet is always with me, I turned away from the list and toward him in my inner vision, just as I had done in the dream. His hands were outstretched toward me, and God's Love streamed into me from his eyes. I placed my hands in his and gazed into his eyes, expressing my love for him. I savored this sacred inner experience. Then we sang HU together for a few moments. I was lifted up to a higher perspective and all my concerns about the list melted away. As I surrendered the day to Prophet he gave me a calm awareness that completing the tasks on the list is not the important thing. The important thing is being aware of his Divine presence and doing everything together. When I opened my eyes and looked at the list from this higher perspective, the items were easy to prioritize. It was also obvious that several of the errands could be combined into an easy travel loop. Prophet helped me see which items could be deleted or postponed and others I wanted to add. The list still seemed to contain more than could be accomplished in one day, but that no longer mattered. I was joyful to be aware of Prophet with me and helping me.

The day went amazingly smooth. People I needed to see were available, and I did not have to search for them. I needed to discuss something with my boss, and as soon as I started to look for him he came right past me and we resolved the issue on the spot! It was evident that Prophet was arranging things ahead of time and making each task easier to accomplish. Throughout the day as other things to do came up, Prophet was helping me know what would be a distraction and a waste of time, and what was important to spend time on. It was freeing to be flexible and not feel tied to completing everything on the list. Some of the most profound blessings of the day came from seemingly chance encounters with other Souls.

I was enjoying this time with Prophet and could see he was making things work out better than I could have planned. It felt really good to cross off each item on the list as we completed it together. Everything on the list was easily accomplished before the day was over. The pearl for me is that it would not have mattered if we had not completed everything. What mattered was Prophet and I were spending quality time together building our relationship of love and trust. This was the answer to my bedtime prayer at the retreat.

When I told my wife that evening about this amazing day and showed her the list with everything crossed off, she said, "Prophet upgraded your to-do list, to a to-be list!" I will never see a to-do list the same again. Since that day my sacred personal relationship with Prophet has been growing more than ever before. I continue to repeat the "Three-Part Prayer" often, and Prophet continues to bless me with experiences that bring us closer together. Through this Divine relationship my life is more abundant with love, joy, peace, strength, and wisdom. I am so grateful for the gift of this dream, and for Prophet showing me that life is so much more than just days filled with things to do. Each twenty-four hour day is filled with opportunities to be led by Spirit and grow closer to God. Thank you Prophet!

Written by Paul Harvey Sandman

38

Reassurance in the ER

*God knows the worries and burdens we carry in our heart.
As a gift of Love He can use anything or anyone to
reassure us we will be all right — even a total stranger.*

This past summer my husband and I found ourselves in the emergency room of a local hospital. Because of a series of recent health issues and the current symptoms he was having the day we went, I was concerned my husband might be having a heart attack. As we sat in the emergency room waiting for the test results, I closed my eyes, sang HU with love, and then quietly prayed. I asked Prophet to please give my husband love in whatever way was best.

A short while later an older gentleman who looked to be in his eighties arrived in the doorway wearing a volunteer's vest. He told us he'd been a volunteer at the hospital for many years and had some health issues of his own which he shared a little bit about. Though it seemed challenging for him to move around the room his demeanor was wonderfully pleasant, cheerful, funny, and kind. The volunteer sat with us awhile. It touched and inspired me that even with his obvious health issues he was still volunteering to bring comfort to others. He and my husband talked and had a very nice conversation, which looked to be uplifting to them both.

Though I was not the one in the hospital bed, the volunteer turned to me a number of times to see if there was anything I needed. The way he continued to ask caught my attention. There wasn't anything I felt I needed, but because he asked I considered coffee or tea, though I did not really want either. What I really wanted but was not aware of until a few minutes later was reassurance. Reassurance my husband was in God's Hands, was receiving the care he needed, and that he would be okay.

After the gentleman sat with us for a little while he stated my husband would heal and get better, that he would be fine again, and to have faith. Oddly, a little earlier the volunteer also shared with us that he himself was not a religious man. Telling us this actually served to make his statement stand out that much more. Having been a hospital volunteer myself I knew his statement about my husband's health was an uncharacteristic thing for a volunteer to say, particularly to a patient in the emergency room who had been admitted for a possible heart attack. But what I noticed about it was the manner in which it was said. There was a solid sureness in the words he spoke, and I knew God had worked through him to give me a message about my husband's health and condition. The reassurance was a huge gift and very much appreciated. I also knew the statement was not just related to this visit, but to the whole series of challenging and interrelated health issues my husband had been dealing with.

After being given this reassurance I felt considerably more relaxed and at ease. God knew my concern, heard what was in my heart, and blessed me with this gift of love! Thank you!

Written by Ruth Levinson

39

Take Me Lord!

Deep within us all is a desire to fully serve God. We know a life of love and service will ultimately bring us the most joy, and Prophet can help us make this dream a reality. Key to this is helping us stay focused when facing one of life's many distractions.

No matter the circumstance Prophet always shares truth and God's Love with me. Over the years he has helped me to slowly remove the many falsehoods I clung to — different masks hiding the real me. The truth is I am Soul, and I am here to serve God. Writing down the first draft for this testimony caused me to sit back in wonder. Slowly the reality of this amazing experience dawned on me and continues to bring a new perspective to my daily life.

It begins at a small gathering of students at Guidance for a Better Life. Prophet was leading us in contemplation — focused time with Prophet and God. I closed my eyes and inwardly saw Prophet gently extend his hands out to me. I felt his love for me, Soul. I held his hands and looked into his eyes, which I love. His inner form was the same as his physical body but made of beautiful golden light which flowed out in all directions from him. I deeply breathed in this Light of God. I felt loved, nurtured, and appreciative of this moment and the opportunity to be with Prophet. We sang HU. I find great joy in being able to purely send love to God by singing HU. Prophet filled me with his love and God's Love, which mingled with my own as I sang each HU. Singing HU was made even sweeter by singing it with Prophet.

After the HU we sat in silence. I was in the room with Prophet and the other students physically, but I was aware of being with Prophet inwardly at God's Ocean too. This is a very pure Heaven, sometimes referred to as the Abode of God. Prophet was a beam of light surrounding me, and I looked up the beam. Then I realized God Himself was aware of me. Very subtly within the beam a clearing was taking place between God and me. In the presence of the Lord I began to submit. Even though I was without body, it felt like I was spreading my arms wide and softly falling backwards. I asked Prophet to help me open up even more to God. "Take me Lord!" I exclaimed. The words came from deep within my being. This meant more than I mentally understood, but I know it was in part a joyful declaration and a request to be allowed to serve God. These were the words of the real me, Soul, revealing my true purpose and my deepest desire.

After being still for awhile I re-experienced part of a dream from the night before. In the dream I was in a dimly lit room full of people. I could barely see. Everybody needed something, and I was being pulled in many directions at once. Then there was a drastic difference. I was in a beam of brilliant light that cut through the atmosphere around me. The contrast between the heavenly light and the dullness of this place was striking. The bright light was Prophet surrounding me, just as he did at God's Ocean. I felt clear, calm, and connected. Now I could navigate through this place safely and confidently with Prophet. Now I knew where to go and what to do next. The way was illuminated by Prophet and my uncertainty was gone. At first I thought the dream was a depiction of where I work, but I think this could also be a representation of life in general. The world is full of potential distractions. There is always one more thing to do; responsibilities, even friends, and family can distract us from the dreams of our heart. We are so loved however, that we are not expected to navigate this journey alone. Prophet is there to help us every step of the way if we also do our part to build and nurture our relationship with him. To serve God more fully I need to stay close to Prophet and let him guide me through life's distractions.

This experience continues to bloom within me as I revisit and contemplate on its meaning. It is bringing new depths of certainty to my understanding of why I am here. I thank you Prophet for being with me always and sharing your love and truth. I love you.

Written by Carmen Snodgrass

40

Seeing God's Blessings

Often there are things that happen in life we could easily write off as lucky coincidences. Learning to recognize them for what they actually are, Divine guidance and protection from a loving God, will bring more gratitude into your life which changes everything for the better.

I had been having trouble seeing at night. My vision would get blurry, and I would see fuzzy halos around lights. I lived on a farm then, and in the summer I would let the horses stay out late into the evening so they could enjoy the grass without the flies and the heat of the day. It was also dark though, and I was having increasing difficulty finding the horses in the field.

It was when I had gone to a doctor for something else that this just happened to come up in conversation. I remember she paused, then almost like you might recount a dream, said she remembered something from way back in medical school about how seeing halos can be a sign of increasing pressure in the eye, glaucoma. This seemed kind of out there at the time, but I went for an eye exam. The test the optometrist did showed my eye pressure as normal, so I thought I was done with that. I wasn't.

A short time later I noticed something on my eyelid. I thought it was just a sty, but it got bigger so I went to an eye doctor. He told me it was something called a chalazion, a growth that can be treated with medicine but often comes back, so he sent me to another eye doctor. When the technician came into the exam room she asked if I was to have my eye pressure checked. I told her I had just had it checked, and I was there for the chalazion thing on my eyelid. For some reason she did the test anyway and left the room.

When the doctor came in he looked pretty serious, and he was not focused on my eyelid. He told me the pressure in my eyes was very high, dangerously high, as in I-could-go-blind high. He put drops in my eyes that would temporarily reduce the pressure, said to continue using them exactly as he instructed, and to call right away if there were any changes. He told me I needed surgery as soon as possible.

I had the surgery, my sight was saved. I was protected. Oh, and that chalazion thing just went away as mysteriously as it had appeared and never came back.

God speaks to us all, all the time, but we often do not recognize the many ways He communicates to us. This time for me it was in the unusual remembrance of a doctor, the seemly illogical decision of a technician, and a completely unrelated eye problem. Maybe you have sometimes wondered if there was something more going on in a situation, beyond the obvious. Perhaps the Divine is guiding you, as it did for me, to something better. I am grateful to recognize the Hand of God in my life throughout the day. It changes everything for the better.

Written by Pam Kisner

41

Soul Knows Truth

You are a spiritual being on a journey home to the Heart of God. You have been created with certain attributes to help guide you during your travels. One of the greatest is the ability of Soul to recognize truth when it hears it.

Before I came to Guidance for a Better Life I knew I was searching for a path to God, but I did not know I was also searching for truth. Even as a child, I knew my parents' church was not for me. I wanted more than to believe, I wanted to know, to experience God for myself.

There is truth that is greater than facts and far beyond opinions. Soul knows truth when it hears it, as the Voice of God sings beneath words to touch the heart. At my first class at Guidance for a Better Life, I heard in Del's voice one of the key truths, that God loves me. It was a survival skills class, but Del wove in spiritual teachings whenever there was interest and opportunity.

This happened often throughout the week, but all I remember now is him saying, "You are loved" over and over. When he spoke, it resonated in my heart like nothing I had ever heard in church. I felt my whole body vibrating with it at times. I've heard people say, "God loves you" countless times. Those who spoke or wrote it surely believed or at least hoped it was true. When Del spoke, I knew it was truth because he knew.

I have experienced God's Love again and again. Over time as I have accepted this truth and more. It was becoming a foundation to build on. No matter what happens or how things appear, I know God loves me. To know from experience is a gift beyond measure. I have been blessed beyond my wildest dreams.

Written by Jean L. Enzbrenner

42

Cleansing and Preparation

Our relationship with God can be so much more than just a few hours on Sunday or twenty minutes during a daily morning contemplation. This sacred relationship is of the greatest value when we move past the boxes of our "spiritual time and practices" and "everything else in life," and instead carry God in our hearts every moment of every day.

Sometimes one awakes from a dream without specific details but the primary message is intact. It was exactly that feeling I got one morning when I awoke and wrote in my dream journal the following: "Then to recognize a dream as cleansing, even though I may not remember the details — that too is cause for rejoicing, giving thanks and praise to God for His work in me, and preparing me further to serve Him." But it was not until a couple of days later that His plan became apparent to me.

It came on a Wednesday morning at the clinic where I work as a physician's assistant, a day we should have been slam-busy and overwhelmed with patients. Somehow the schedule cleared enough for me to have a few minutes and I got a nudge out of the blue to call my brother in Missouri. And it was perfect timing. He happened to be at work and was able to unload some stuff he was concerned about. I was there to listen, and in the listening I heard him sort through the facts and share something with me that would be helpful to both of us later on. The Holy Spirit had been at work to arrange events and schedules so when I did follow the nudge, the blessings unfolded with ripple effects on all sides. I had followed the inner nudge to call my brother just when he really needed to talk to me.

"Draw nigh to God, and He will draw nigh to you." I have quoted that scripture to my brother before, but if I have learned anything from Del, it is that we do not have to wait for a retreat to draw nigh to God and to deepen our relationship with Him. In the past I did my spiritual exercises in the morning at home and then left for work, leaving that relationship behind and jumping headlong into my job, forgetting God in the process. What spiritual progress I did make was by fits and starts, which could be exhausting at times. With the help and encouragement of Del Hall III, I finally realized my morning only time for contemplation was not real nourishment for Soul but more like spiritual fast food, providing a rush but nothing of sustenance. Prophet has helped me see my prayers as a more personal way of addressing God with trust and confidence those prayers are heard; and to take my relationship with Him throughout the day relying more on His guidance and protection, sustaining me at the same time. It took time and effort on my part to leave behind the old way of prayer as a routine to follow in favor of more complete reliance on God.

So I return to the dream of cleansing and preparation I was blessed with, and give thanks I am even aware of nudges. I was now prepared to be a coworker for God. Because I stayed spiritually nourished throughout the day, and not just in the morning, God was able to use me to bless my brother. I was aware of the nudge to call him just when he really needed to talk, and get some things off his chest. It is this trust and awareness that have been nurtured over twenty years by my relationship with both the inner and outer Prophet. In looking back over this time I realize I have never felt judgment or condemnation, but rather the unconditional love and mercy of the Heavenly Father. My commitment has been strengthened on all sides to continue my part in this process; how could I not be grateful for this blessing?

Written by James Kinder

43

Shower in the Light

Those who have the eyes to see God's Love and guidance will recognize it all around them, which makes life a greater joy to live. Those who do not — can learn. It's in your core nature as Soul to recognize God's Love in even the seemingly little things of life.

To see the Hand of God, Spirit at work in our lives all around us is a huge blessing and an upgrade in living everyday life. The daily grind, including all the details of a typical day, would just be very mundane without the knowledge of the Divine Hand behind it all. Learning about and using the spiritual tools I was taught at Guidance for a Better Life by Del has opened up a new life for me and my understanding of the world I live in.

God can bless us any time He knows we need encouragement, or maybe even just because he loves us. On one such occasion I was blessed to receive a gift from God at the end of a workday.

I had worked late one evening and had a long drive home. When I did get home I was in need of a shower, but the electricity was out on the second floor of our townhouse where the shower was located. Sort of grumbling under my breath I said, "I don't want to take a shower in the dark." So before I lit some candles that were set out for just such a situation I thought I would just try the light switch one more time — like I had done almost every time I passed the bathroom since the power had gone out. This time the lights did come on and I was really surprised. With jaw-dropping awe I immediately jumped into the shower and took care of business as fast as I could. I was kind of giddy at the thought of having the electricity work because I knew it should not be working.

Finishing up in the bathroom I shut the lights off, and you know I had to try turning the lights on again. So I flicked on the light switch, and the lights did not work again until maintenance came and rewired part of the second floor. Wow, what a blessing that God knew about a need I had. A small detail, but God gave me a lot of encouragement to keep on keeping on. Some people may have thought it was just a fluke, a glitch in the light switch or something of that nature, but I knew better. It was one of the countless ways the Hand of God is at work in my life.

I have also learned an experience such as my second floor needing to be rewired can sometimes be taken to a deeper level and considered an awake dream. When comparing the second floor rewiring to my personal life, I can see how it directly applies to my old ways of thinking. My way of thinking was causing problems in my everyday life. I was in the process of using the spiritual tools I had been taught, while also asking the Divine for help to get my patterns of thinking rewired — during the same time period the rewiring was needed in my townhouse.

The events happening simultaneously are no coincidence, but an example of the Hand of God at work. These events can be better understood by learning the "Language of the Divine" as taught by Del. My spiritual tools contributed greatly to a new way of thinking, which I am still working on. If you are tired of a mundane way of life and in need of a new way of thinking, maybe the spiritual tools could work for you too.

Written by Sam Spitale

44

Keep My Heart Always

When we joyfully and completely give our heart to God we gain the Kingdom of Heaven in the here and now — right here, in this world. This loving surrender is natural for Soul and not a one-time thing. We can renew this commitment with every breath.

Sunday morning during a winter weekend retreat, a small group of Prophet's students gathered in his sunny great room. Seated with eyes closed, we were silent at first. In that silence we each had the opportunity to meet with Prophet in the inner worlds. I saw the two of us standing face to face, holding hands, looking into each other's eyes. We were silent but my heart spoke, asking for his help to better "seek first the Kingdom of Heaven" every day, in everything I do.

After several minutes Del led the group in singing HU. Inwardly, still hand in hand with Prophet, I sang this beautiful sound, noticing the blend of our voices as well as individual voices within the group. Time seemed to stand still as we sang, sending our love to God. Suddenly an aspect of God appeared before me in my inner vision, a huge golden ball of light — alive, powerful, emanating love and mercy. All I wanted to do was send love back to God as purely as possible. I asked Prophet to bring me closer to God. We walked together toward the light, and as we did I felt an important shift in myself: I didn't just want to send God love, I wanted to give Him love. I wanted to give God my heart, my whole heart, and I wanted nothing more than for Him to accept it from me. As we neared this massive ball of living, golden light — this aspect of God — I knelt and offered my heart to God with both hands. Holding it out I looked down and saw it was also made of golden light, with the same characteristics of the Light of God. Two Hands emerged from the Light and accepted my heart — accepted it instantly. I felt like God had been waiting for me to come to Him, ready to accept my heart the moment I offered it. He took it gently and placed it inside Himself, and as He did I was immediately filled with peace and a sense of equilibrium — I felt balanced, clear, and relaxed. My heart flooded with gratitude for God's Love and mercy, for His palpable compassion. I found myself crying happy, grateful tears, and my voice was choked with joyful emotion so I could not sing for a few moments.

After we stopped singing, we sat with eyes closed in the still, sunny great room. Prophet spoke to me inwardly, "The only way forward is to let God keep your heart always." Always. All ways. I reflected on these words and on what had just taken place during the HU song. I have always loved God, but today during this HU song I had deepened my commitment. I have heard the expression "sweet surrender," and this was what I had done, willingly and joyfully. A most welcome, sweet surrender to God. I am a child of God, made of His dynamic, beautiful Light. In fully giving God my heart I am doing what is most natural to the real me, Soul. While still living in a physical body I am able to come home to God, to my true Home. It is where I am happiest and can truly be myself.

Every time I go back and relive this experience of Prophet taking me to God and of Him accepting my heart, I remember this is one way I can seek first the Kingdom of Heaven. And I feel like I get a chance to consciously give God my heart again, renewing and solidifying my commitment to let Him keep my heart always.

Written by Joan Clickner

45

The "Little Things" in Life

Life is so much sweeter for those who recognize and are
grateful for God's Love in their life. It is in everything,
from the grandest expanse to the smallest of details.

While looking up at the stars on a clear winter
night in the mountains, I was struck by the
magnificence of God's creation — a primal
experience shared with many other Souls since
the beginning of human consciousness in this
world. As I began to sing HU the inner Prophet
reminded me of an experience I was given
during a weeklong retreat. During a spiritual
exercise I was shown universes being created,
filling me with overwhelming awe of the
supremacy of our Creator. I was then
immediately shown an indigo butterfly receiving
nourishment from a white daisy with a golden
center, again filling me with overwhelming awe.
Why was I given this experience during the
retreat and reminded of it this night? Before

going to sleep I prayed I would have clarity to know the lessons Prophet offered me.

The next morning waking up warm in my bed I felt excited to start the day. I knew in this day, like all days, there were many discoveries waiting to be shown to me by Prophet. I knew my prayer for clarity, like all our prayers, was heard. From the moment my feet touched the cold floor I was filled with gratitude for all the seemingly "little things" in life. First, I was grateful I woke up and could feel my feet. Next, I had a kitchen to go into, a wood stove with wood to stoke, clean water and a way to make it hot for tea, anticipating seeing my wife when she wakes up, going out on the porch to feel the sun warm my face; moment to moment throughout the day seeing God's Hand in everything, personally guiding and providing for each of us.

From creating universes to giving nourishment to a butterfly, one not greater or less than the other, are all gifts of God's Love. These gifts are freely given to all of us, no exceptions. Look for them, accept them, be grateful and you will know how much God loves YOU and wants to help you in all aspects of your life. Even the seemingly big challenges will become opportunities to learn and know how much you are loved. Pray for "the eyes to see" and you will recognize God's Love and blessings in your life.

Written by Terry Kisner

46

Truth Uncovered

You are so much more than your physical body or any of the labels you could place on yourself. You are first and foremost Soul, an eternal spiritual being created by God with love. If you are blessed to experience this truth firsthand for yourself, you will truly know God loves you just the way you are.

Sometimes we have an experience with God that is pivotal to our growth, a precious moment we hold sacred in our hearts that we will never forget. A moment that transforms us so much we can never see ourselves the way we were before that precious experience. This story is one of those moments for me.

It was the October 3-Day Retreat of 2013. I had been having some inner struggles with self-doubt, self-acceptance, and wondering if God really could love me the way I was. I didn't even know if I loved me just the way I was. We sat in the Beach House, our sacred classroom. It was evening, and even though the wind was blowing cold outside it was warm inside and there was a comforting feeling inside the classroom. Del, the Prophet, offered us the opportunity to be blessed by the Divine and join him for a spiritual experience. As I sat with my eyes closed Prophet led us in a HU song to God. I began to feel lighter, and as I surrendered to the Divine, I felt God's pure Love pouring into me and filling me with attributes such as strength and a trust not only in Him but in myself as well.

I was standing in a huge column of God's Light and Love. I felt completely safe and secure bathed in this love. Prophet showed me myself. I looked how I know myself to look when I look into the mirror; I saw my physical body. Prophet shared with us that we could shed our outer body, our "earth suit," in the same fashion we would take off a garment of clothing. Prophet helped me shed this outer sheath like a jacket, and I watched it fall away from me. Then without pausing he brought me up to the first Heaven, also referred to as the Astral plane. The part of myself I could now see looked like the physical body I knew as myself, but it was lighter, glowed more, and had a translucency my physical body did not have.

While I did not see Prophet at that moment, I was acutely aware of his strong presence and knew it was only with his guidance and help I was being raised in consciousness to other planes; to higher and higher Heavens. I have read in scripture, 2 Corinthians 12:2 KJV, where Saint Paul spoke of "a man caught up to the third heaven," and this was what I was being given the opportunity to experience for myself. Prophet brought me to the next Heaven, the Causal plane, and on the way up I shed my Astral body and watched it fall away, revealing my Causal body which was even lighter and brighter than my Astral body had been. We continued our upward journey in this beam of God's Light, and as we raised up to each Heaven I shed each corresponding body: my Astral body, my Causal body, my Mental body, and finally I shed my body from the Etheric plane to reveal my true self, Soul. I was a blindingly bright ball of God's Light and Sound.

Prophet asked us to look at our true self. I saw something so beautiful, so pure, and so refined. My brightness and light was astoundingly breathtaking. This is how God made me, this is the real me! I felt no worries, no fears, no concerns, nor insecurities as I basked in this moment of truth experienced. An overwhelming knowing came over me and sank into my heart; God truly does love me. I knew God Himself was placing this truth directly into my open heart: "God loves me just the way I am." I looked at myself, and I loved what I beheld. How could I not love such a precious, beautiful Soul? How could I not love something God uniquely and purposely made? I then understood that those garments, those light bodies from each Heaven of God covered up my true self, Soul. These light-bodies, layer over layer, had hidden from me the most beautiful truth of all, that I am Soul. This experience completely shattered the previous perception I had of myself.

I wish I could fully convey to you how precious and amazing it was to see myself in my true form as Soul. It was liberating, it was strengthening, and it was awe-inspiring. It freed me from the restrictive confines of how this physical world dictates to me daily that I was a woman, a wife, a mother, a daughter, a worker, and a washer of sippy cups. I am no longer bound by some idea of who I am based on my appearance, or what I do, or my physical belongings. These physical trappings cannot even touch the sacredness of my true Divine nature.

I am so eternally grateful to have been given such a loving gift, to see with clarity how limitless and breathtaking my true self is as Soul. I now have a new image of myself. No wonder I had a hard time loving myself; I had never truly experienced the real me. Do you desire to experience your true self?

Written by Ahna Spitale

47

A Dream Teaching on Real Freedom

Some people ask, "Why does God allow suffering?" It is not that God allows suffering; it is that God allows us the freedom to make our own choices and our choices have consequences. This is a higher gift of love than taking away our freedom to keep us safe would be, for we learn from our choices — the good ones and the bad. This truth is hard to fully understand and accept if looked at through the lens of "we only live a single lifetime."

One night I was home in my bed preparing for sleep after a weeklong retreat. I began to sing two spiritually charged words, Prophet and HU. Before singing I had a soft intent to learn more about some topics we had discussed at retreats this year. One of the topics was the spiritual Law of Unity, which allows one to see both the big picture and the details of a situation; a higher view from many angles. I also hoped to learn more about how to allow myself to genuinely feel concern for others, which I do, without impinging on their free will or losing my peace because of their choices. I wanted to accept more of the freedom being offered to me as a student of Prophet.

With this gentle intent I began to drift off to sleep. I awoke within a dream where I met Prophet in a sort of in-between world. We were in a blank space together, and I was encompassed in a dark blue light. I could see stars and galaxies all around us. Prophet extended his hands and I accepted them. We went on a journey through the many worlds of God. Del, in his Soul body, raised me up above the worlds of God, and I could see an overview of a vastness that is inexplicable. There was no beginning or end to the spheres within spheres of galaxies and universes. I knew I was viewing as much as I could of God's creation, the big picture. In the blink of an eye we were walking through a scene that felt like a sort of "hell." It was a place where there were extreme poverty, grief, and oppression in the deepest sense. As we walked past these scenes I saw an abundant display of cruelty and ignorance, most too graphic to describe.

In one scene a father and mother were injecting themselves and their child with heroine. Some might wonder how God could allow this. A part of me wanted to stay here in this place and help these Souls, but how? A prayer entered my heart, and I asked Prophet to extend whatever grace he could to these Souls. Whatever you can do for them, I pleaded. Just then a golden light flowed from Prophet into my heart and out to those Souls. A sense of deep peace flowed into me, and I knew I could move on. I knew that I had to. It was not my place to stay there. They had been given whatever they needed, and I had peace not knowing or needing to know what that was.

"God gives Soul freedom to choose what it wants to do. Free will is a gift, and if we pray for others to do what we want them to do or what we think they should do we are violating their freedom," said Prophet in his radiant majesty. As we continued through this nightmare I wished every Soul well. I prayed they would realize the true dreams of their heart. I also surrendered the outcome of my prayers to Prophet. "Thy will be done, not mine." Just then I heard the words "They too are loved by God, no less than these Souls." Prophet pointed and I looked.

Now we were in a very high plane or mansion of God. There was lightness and peace everywhere I looked. A golden light surrounded us, and we seemed to be in an ocean resort. Everyone was happy here. There were Souls serving other Souls and they seemed genuinely joyful to be able to serve others. This place looked like where people typically go on vacation to be served, but ironically the Souls here were servers. They were servants of God, the happiest of all Souls. This was such a drastic change from where we had just been. I wondered what the difference was between the Souls in the hellish place and the Souls here in what seemed to be a type of Heaven. An answer came; perhaps it was their choices. The Souls dwelling in the lower consciousness were making more self-indulgent choices, and the ones dwelling in the higher consciousness were making more selfless choices. Choices had been made in prior lifetimes as well as this current one. The circumstances they were in were not random. There was Divine perfection to everything. I could see it. This gave me a profound sense of peace.

Each Soul had a syllabus and was learning and growing even though it appeared some of the lessons were very harsh. These courses took place over many lifetimes and on many planes, not just the physical. I was shown this big picture, an overview of what real freedom looks like in this dream experience. It was the opposite of what we are told here on Earth. Society, for the most part, teaches us to attain status and power so we can have others wait on us. In my dream teaching with Prophet, the Souls serving God and His creation were the happiest and freest. They felt God's Love the most and were able to pass it on. They were able to move about God's many spheres of existence and were not overly attached to anything in any of the vast worlds.

When I woke up from this dream experience I thought of the Bible scripture "cast thy burden upon the Lord, and he shall sustain thee." Psalm 55:22 KJV It doesn't say don't care, but rather cast your care to the Prophet of our times. In doing so, I did not become overly attached to saving the hurting Souls I saw. If I would have done that, I myself would have been trapped in that place. By consciously walking with Prophet and giving my prayers to him, I knew exactly what to do and what not to do. I was not being asked to get involved. I knew my prayer was heard and answered. I could literally see the blessings I prayed for being offered. What I learned was that the Souls dwelling in the higher Heavens were not loved more than those in the lower worlds. They were each loved equally. The Souls dwelling in the higher planes had graduated to different lessons and experiences via their choices. I believe my detached prayers, my assuming the Prophet would know what was best, allowed me to stay above the fray but still be helpful. There was a balance. Helping others is about giving ourselves over to God through His Prophet, so we can be used as instruments for Him to uplift rather than get pulled into situations by strong emotions and attachment to outcomes.

I still felt sadness for the Souls I encountered having the harsher lessons, but I was not overcome by it. I could cast my care into the loving hands of Prophet, who knows those Souls better than I do. There is emotional balance, joy, stability, peace, and freedom in that. I am a sensitive Soul. There was a time when I tried to numb myself to the sorrows of the world. That brought me unhappiness. My relationship with Prophet gives me the freedom to feel for others without losing my balance or peace. I have better boundaries. I no longer hurt myself in order to help others. When I am genuinely moved for another I ask: "Prophet if there is something I can do, let me know how I can help. If not, whatever you can do for them, your will be done, not mine." On this dream journey I learned that every Soul is heading back to the Heart of God eventually. There were many planes and certainly more than one lifetime per Soul. The world that looked like hell was not a fixed state. The Souls there would not be there indefinitely. Every Soul is loved by our Creator. None were alone. The Prophet's presence, although unbeknownst to some of them, was there. Within the many mansions of God are His children learning and growing, until one day they make their way to their true Home in the Heart of God. With this comes real freedom.

Written by Tash Canine

48

Heart of a Child

Our children may be physically young, but as Soul they are just as old as us. They too have access to the higher truths of God and in many ways have less mental hang-ups between themselves and the recognition of those truths. It would be a beautiful thing if parents could help their children grow into the responsibility of adulthood while maintaining a childlike openness to God.

It really is amazing to be a dad to my young children, especially from the perspective of a student at Guidance for a Better Life and Prophet Del Hall III. There are truths that have taken me twenty years to learn, that my children know instinctively. They know there is a living God who loves them unconditionally and who communicates with them daily. They know giving is a key to happiness. Witnessing this on a regular basis has blessed me and fills me with a childlike sense of wonder as these Souls play and grow, fuss and argue, and otherwise figure out their way in this physical world. They amaze me daily. One day they will say something that blows me away and the next moment they will act very age-appropriate, like crying because their favorite pajamas which have been worn for the past three days need to be washed, and all the alternative jammies are "just not the same!"

One night at bedtime when my eldest son Liam was two and a half, he called out for me. Often he wanted an additional "one last hug" or he was not quite ready to go to sleep and was trying to coax another bedtime story out of me. I entered his room, which was decorated with a hand-painted mural of an Octopus's Garden, with a friendly eight-legged sentinel watching over his sister's crib. Liam lay on his back with a far-off gaze on his face. He said something in a strong but quiet voice. I was not sure I had heard him correctly so I moved closer and asked him to repeat what he had said. "Prophet is in my heart," he said simply, his hand over his heart in testimony.

His face transcended the moment, the setting of his bedroom, and our roles as father and son in this lifetime. There was an ancientness about him that contrasted with his youthful countenance. He did not speak to me as my son, or as a cute little boy, or even as a human. He spoke to me as Soul, the Divine essence created by God and placed in these physical bodies for the simple purpose of growing in its ability to give and receive love. There was reverence in his soft voice that melted away my fatigue and the various concerns of my long day. I leaned over and listened intently. "Feel, Daddy," he said moving my hand over his chest. "Right here. Feel it?"

Divine truth poured out freely as I witnessed this beautiful Soul connect the Divine and eternal presence of Prophet with his very heartbeat. This was not something I had taught him. He was not regurgitating something he had overheard his parents say. This was truth he brought with him, as Soul, into this body and was simply connecting it to his immediate reality: God is alive and is always with us — as close as our heartbeat — in the form of His chosen Prophet. As Soul, we all know this. When you slow down and listen with the heart of a child, you too can hear the beating of God's Love for you.

Written by Chris Comfort

49

Building Divine Relationships

❦

Regardless of how far we've come on our spiritual journey — there is always more. Nowhere is this more evident than in the amount of God's Love available for us. It is infinite, and as we are able to accept even more it will be showered upon us.

Guidance for a Better Life offers a five-part Keys to Spiritual Freedom course of study. The third retreat in this series is titled, "Building Divine Relationships" and is taught by Prophet Del Hall III. Divine relationships can be with God, the Voice of God (sometimes called the Light and Sound of God or the Holy Spirit), God's Prophet, or with Soul — your true self. Under Prophet Hall's loving guidance I had an experience at this retreat that could easily be the highlight of a lifetime. It is one I will never forget that held great significance and helped me gain a greater capacity to love.

Before singing HU, Prophet asked us to think of something we were grateful for specifically from that day, and then to ask for an experience of some type that would help me build my relationship with the Divine, and then promise to be receptive to whatever blessings I was given. I began by being grateful for something that happened early in the day at home and my thoughts just flowed from one moment to the next. Without intending to do so, I ended up going through my day, step by step, and saw God's Hand in everything I did, and I felt gratitude for it all. We began singing HU, and an amazing experience followed. After singing HU it took me a while to take it all in. I had a hard time finding the words to describe what had happened.

In my journal I wrote: "Oh my gosh — LOVE. My heart is just bursting and overflowing with love. It began in my heart, love pouring out so strong, fueled by the gratitude I felt every step of my day — I couldn't just stop at one thing. The love flowed out of me to you Dear God, but it was unlike anything I had ever felt before. A kind of dam broke, a wall or resistance of some type was cleared by your Grace and love poured out of me. It felt strong, beautiful, and uplifting.

Your Divine Spirit beckoned me closer with Its Heavenly music, eventually engulfing me into the sound. I felt love, indistinguishable now whether coming out of me to you Lord, or from you to me. It was our love, the love of our relationship. I may have experienced this in a very real way before, but perhaps I am feeling it in a more true sense tonight as whatever hurts or pains I had numbed myself to were healed, and the protective walls I had built around my heart crumbled in the light of your security, comfort, and magnificent Love. I cried and cried the most beautiful tears I have ever felt. It was almost hard to breathe because the feeling of awe from the beauty of it took my breath away. As I write, even now, the tears keep flowing. "Rapture" is the word that is in my heart. This love I feel is incredible! It has been there, but not like this. The love in me has been strong and very much there, building all these years, but now it is flowing, and I can feel it more than ever tonight. Oh my gosh — the tears just keep coming. It is amazing. Thank you!!!"

This incredible experience took me by surprise. It helped me build upon my Divine relationships in part by showing me the depth of what was already there and then taking me even farther with realizations that followed. I know to my core that I love God and have felt it. I know God and His Prophet love me, and I have felt and experienced this love in many beautiful ways, and yet the degree and intensity of what I felt in this experience knocked my socks off. There truly is always more...wow! It is not random, of course. I see a seamless progression over time from retreat to home to retreat, and a continuous flow of God's Grace and Love through truth, insights, healings, experiences with the light and sound, direct interaction with aspects of the Divine, and being blessed moment to moment with added clarity, purification, and more being in Prophet's presence. My heart is filled with gratitude and appreciation for God's Prophet, and the life of abundant love he has brought me to living.

Written by Lorraine Fortier

50

The Throne of God

As beautiful as this Earth is, it is but a pale shadow of the inner Heavenly worlds. Those fortunate to be taken there spiritually by Prophet know this well. Even so, it is in this physical world where we live and love and serve. Cherish your time here.

In the winter of 2012 I was blessed to kneel before the mighty Throne of God. While I was singing HU, the Prophet of our times Del Hall III, raised me spiritually from my body to the heights of Heaven. I perceived it as an Ocean, where the rhythmic waves were not composed of water but of endless Love and Grace. Prophet led me, swimming through the shining waves. Light came from all directions, below the water and above, filling me with gentle peace and joy. As we swam farther from the shore the light grew whiter and more bright.

We crossed into a realm beyond description. The light around us flowed together to create a room, with walls and all within it made of the same pure, dancing light. There were others in the room, all kneeling down in reverence to the Lord. I knelt as well, with joy, so grateful to have reached this sacred place. Beneath my knees there lay a carpet made of light leading to the Throne of God Himself. My eyes moved along this path until they came to rest upon His shining Throne.

And there appeared the figure of the Lord. I know what my eyes could see was but a fraction of His true, eternal self. With eyes so filled with Love, He gazed out from His Throne and spoke a single sound. At first it seemed to be the faintest whisper. Yet from His lips came forth such Love and Power, in all directions, that I'm sure it reached the boundaries of creation. The loving power of His Voice rushed through me like a mighty wind. It stripped away impurity and left the real me: my true, eternal self. As His Voice kept moving through me, two words came to mind: duty and responsibility.

As the vision faded, the song of HU resumed within me. Slowly my eyes opened, and I could see this world for the shadow that it is, a quickly fading flame beneath the greater worlds above. Yet in this world lay the duty and responsibility.

These tasks are not a burden, but a joy and blessing to fulfill. With each day comes the chance to make this blessing a reality. To live each moment kneeling, in my inner heart of hearts, before the Throne of God. To live as Soul, the real me, my true eternal self, and follow Prophet's guidance throughout my daily life. To do this is a privilege. It makes my life a joy to live and fills it with abundance.

God always has a living Prophet here on Earth to help us, to raise us into Heaven and guide our daily lives. Seek truth with a pure heart, and you will find the Prophet of our times. He is the Living Word, a link between the Throne of God and man.

Written by David Hughes

Guidance for a Better Life
Our Story

My Father's Journey

God always has a living Prophet on Earth to teach His Ways and accomplish His will. My father, Del Hall III, is currently God's true Prophet fully raised up and ordained by God Himself. He was not always a Prophet, nor did he even know what a Prophet was, but God had a plan

Prophet Del Hall III

for him like He has for all of His children. Over many years through many life experiences, God had begun to prepare my father for his future assignment, mostly unbeknownst to him. Everything he experienced in his life from the joys to the sadness helped prepare him for his future role as Prophet.

My dad grew up in California and was a decent student but a better athlete. He received an appointment to the United States Naval Academy in Annapolis, Maryland where he later met my mother. They were married two days after he graduated and received his commission as an officer. After a short tour on a Navy ship deployed to Vietnam, he went to flight training school and became a Navy fighter pilot. While attending flight school in Pensacola, Florida he also earned a Master of Science Degree and had the first of his three children, a son. After flight school he was stationed in a fighter squadron on the East Coast, where he and my mom began investing in real estate, adding to their family with the birth of two daughters. Following this tour of duty he was assigned as a jet flight instructor in Texas, after which, his time in the Navy was finished. He was a natural pilot and loved his time in the sky, but it was time to move on.

So far in life he had no real concern for, or even thought much about God, religion, or spiritual matters in general. He lived life fully. He raised his family. He traveled. He invested and became an entrepreneur starting and growing highly successful businesses in diverse fields ranging from real estate to aerospace consulting. Years before however, a seed had been planted when God's eternal teachings were introduced to him in his late teens, and while it did not show outwardly, the truth in these teachings spoke to his heart. My dad might not have been giving much thought about God up to this point in his life, but God was definitely thinking about him and the future He had planned for him. Like an acorn destined to become a mighty oak, the seed that lay dormant in his heart would someday be stirred to life. Through all his life experiences, both "good" and "bad," God would be preparing him for his future role as His Prophet.

When God decided it was time, He called my dad to Him. He did this by shutting down the world of financial security my dad had built. Over a period of two years all of his businesses were wound down and dissolved. What seemed like security turned out to be an illusion. Financial success had not provided true security. He now had failed businesses and a failing marriage and was trying to fix things without God's help, principles, or guidance. As painful as this time in his life was, it was yet another step towards the glorious life of service awaiting my father. God was removing him from the world my dad had created and furthering him along his path to his future role as Prophet.

After his marriage ended and his businesses wound down, he started fresh by going out west to give flying lessons near Lake Mead, Nevada. While living in Nevada my dad was reintroduced to the eternal teachings of God he first learned of as a teenager twenty-three years earlier, and though they resonated with him at the time, his priorities were different back then. Now, his serious training could begin. He started having very clear experiences with the Holy Spirit and noticed there was a familiarity with these teachings and experiences. He embraced the long hours of instruction, which often lasted until sunrise, and was receptive to the personal spiritual experiences he was given. This began an intense period of study and desire for spiritual truth that continues to this day. Some of his most profound and meaningful experiences during this time were with past Prophets of old. They came to him spiritually in contemplations and dreams. He learned of their roles in history and how they were raised up and ordained by God directly. He began to realize they were training him but was not clear why. A few times his experiences led him to believe he was in training to be a future Prophet. However, that revelation made no sense to him because he felt he was an imperfect person who made mistakes and had failures. He thought of the past and current Prophets of God as perfected Souls, not imperfect like he felt he was. Why would God choose him for such a role? He did not feel qualified.

Besides being introduced to God's teachings while he was out west, my father was blessed to meet his current wife Lynne. Returning to the East Coast, my father and Lynne moved into a small cabin on land he had acquired before his businesses shut down. This was a major change in his life, but it felt deeply right within him. He began to remember a desire to live like this as a child; from early childhood my dad found clarity and peace in nature. He had forgotten about this until now, but God had not and made this dream a reality. In addition to being their home, these beautiful, three-hundred-plus acres of land in the Blue Ridge Mountains would eventually become the location for the Guidance for a Better Life retreat center. The perfection of my father's experiences from earlier in his life in real estate, providing the land for his next step in life, speaks to the perfection of God's plan. One of many many examples I could list.

For many years my dad took wilderness skills courses around the country. He specialized in the study of wild edible and medicinal plants, tracking, and awareness skills, and authored articles for publication. Inspired to help folks feel more comfortable in the outdoors, my dad and Lynne began the Nature Awareness School in 1990. Classes were focused on teaching awareness and the primitive living skills needed to enjoy the woods and survive in them if necessary. An amazing thing happened within those first few years though; students began to experience aspects of God in very personal and dramatic ways. Somewhat like my dad's experience out west, they found that stepping away from their daily routine and the hustle of life, if even for a few days, created space for Spirit to do Its work. Whether they were enjoying the beauty of the Virginia wilderness and tranquility of the school grounds or relaxing by the pond, he found students' hearts opened, and they became more receptive to the Divine Hand that is always reaching out to Its children.

More and more the discourse during wilderness classes shifted to the meanings of dreams, personal growth, finding balance in life, and experiences the students were having with the Voice of God in Its many forms. An increase of spiritual retreats was offered to fulfill the demand and over time became the predominant class offerings; the wilderness survival skills classes eventually fading away completely. The name "Nature Awareness School" seemed to be less fitting for what was actually being taught now and in February 2019 my father changed the name of the retreat center to Guidance for a Better Life.

Throughout this time my father's training and spiritual study continued. My father reached mastership and was ordained by God on July 7, 1999 but he was still not yet Prophet, more was required. On October 22, 2012, twenty-five years since his full-time intensive training had begun, God ordained him as His chosen Prophet, and He has continued to raise him up further since. God works through my father in very direct and beneficial ways for his students. Hundreds and hundreds of students for more than thirty years have received God's eternal teachings through my father's instruction and mentoring. They have had personal experiences with the Divine which have transformed and greatly blessed their lives. My father's greatest joy is being used by God as a servant to share God's ways and truths with thirsty Souls and hungry seekers. In addition to mountaintop retreats, my father continues to spread God's ways and teachings that so greatly blessed his life and the lives of his loved ones in many ways, including his books and videos.

Maybe you are at a turning point in your life and looking for direction. Maybe you have a knowing there is more to life but not sure what that might be or how to find it. Or, maybe you are simply drawn to what you read and hear in our stories. God speaks to our hearts and calls each of us in many different ways. Like my father's journey demonstrates, it doesn't matter where you started or the twists, turns, or seeming dead-ends your life has taken; God wants us to know Him more fully, and for us to know our purpose within His creation. He wants us to experience His Love regardless of our religious path or lack thereof. He always has a living Prophet here on Earth to help us accomplish His desire for us — to show us the way home to Him and to experience more abundance in our lives while we are still living here on Earth. God's Prophet today is my father, Del Hall III. You have the opportunity to grow spiritually through God's teachings which Prophet shares. His guidance for a better life is available for you — please accept it.

Written by Del Hall IV

My Son, Del Hall IV

My son, Del Hall IV, joined Guidance for a Better Life as an instructor after fifteen years of in-class training with me, his father. He helped develop the five-step Keys to Spiritual Freedom Study Program and facilitates the first two courses in the

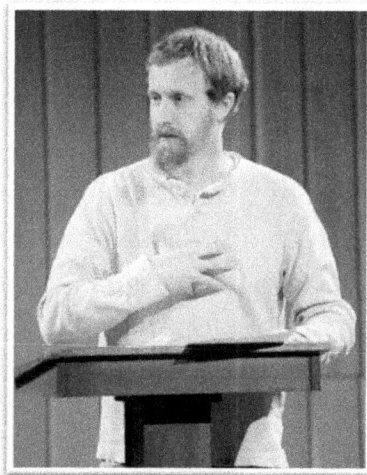

Del Hall IV

program: Step One "Tools to Recognize Divine Guidance" and Step Two "Understanding Divine Guidance." Del also teaches people about the rich history of dream study and how to better recall their own dreams during the Dream Study Workshops, which he hosts around the country. He is qualified to step in and facilitate any of my retreats should the need arise.

Del authored the book *God is in the Garden*, a priceless book of wisdom in the form of parables. Through stories of everyday events of life on the mountain Del shares profound insights into the nature of God and life that are infused with his natural humor and unique perspective.

Del is also Vice President of Marketing and helps with everything required to get the "good news" from Guidance for a Better Life out to hungry seekers: everything from book publishing, blogging, and posting on social media outlets. He is co-author and book cover designer for many of our, thus far, twenty published books.

My son loves the opportunity to work on creative projects for Guidance for a Better Life. From a very early age he has been an artist and loved creating artwork in multiple mediums. He was accepted into gifted art programs in Virginia Beach, Virginia and then after high school graduation he attended the School of the Museum of Fine Arts in Boston. He is now a nationally exhibited artist and his *Paintings of the Light and Sound of God* are in over two hundred public and private collections. One of the greatest joys of the painting process for Del is using his paintings as an opportunity to share with others the inspiration behind them, God's

Love and his experiences with the Light and Sound of God, the Holy Spirit, in contemplation and in waking life.

Del lives on the retreat center property in the Blue Ridge Mountains of Virginia with his wife where they raised and homeschooled my three grandchildren. Recently he helped me with an extensive renovation and update for the three hand-built log cabins on retreat center property originally used for advanced spiritual retreats. He loves woodworking, tending to his vegetable garden, pruning his fruit trees, and helping maintain the beautiful three-hundred acres of retreat center property for students to enjoy. There is always something that needs attention on the land and Del is always up to the challenge. He loves to travel and spends his free time enjoying this beautiful country with his family in their RV.

My son has had multiple brain surgeries starting when he was seventeen years old for a recurring brain tumor. He credits God for surviving and thriving all this time when most with his condition do not. He looks to the sunrise every day with gratitude for yet another chance at life. With that chance he desires to help me share the love and teachings of God that have so blessed our lives. I pray to God daily thanking Him for my son's good health.

Written by Prophet Del Hall

What is the Role of God's Prophet?

An introductory understanding of God's handpicked and Divinely trained Prophet is necessary to fully benefit from reading this book. God ALWAYS has a living Prophet of His choice on Earth. He has a physical body with a limited number of students, but the inner spiritual side of Prophet is limitless. Spiritually he can help countless numbers of Souls all over the world, no matter what religion or path they are on — even if that is no path at all. He teaches the ways of God and shares the Light and Sound of God. He delivers the living Word of God. Prophet can teach you physically as well as through dreams, and he can lift you into the Heavens of God. He offers protection, peace, teachings, guidance, healing, and love.

Each of God's Prophets throughout history has a unique mission. One may only have a few students with the sole intent to keep God's teachings and truth alive. God may use another to change the course of history. God's Prophets are usually trained by both the current and former Prophets. The Prophet is tested and trained over a very long period of time. The earlier Prophets are physically gone but teach the new Prophet in the inner spiritual worlds. This serves two main purposes: the trainee becomes very adept at spiritual travel and gains wisdom from those in whose shoes he will someday walk. This is vital training because the Prophet is the one who must safely prepare and then take his students into the Heavens and back.

There are many levels of Heaven, also called planes or mansions. Saint Paul once claimed to know a man who went to the third Heaven. Actually it was Paul himself that went, but the pearl is, if there is a third Heaven, it presumes a first and second Heaven also exist. The first Heaven is often referred to as the Astral plane. Even on just that one plane of existence there are over one hundred sub-planes. This Heaven is where most people go after passing, unless they receive training while still here in their physical body. Without a guide who is trained properly in the ways of God a student could misunderstand the intended lesson and become confused as to what is truth. The inner worlds are enormous compared to the physical worlds. They are very real and can be explored safely when guided by God's Prophet.

Part of my mission is to share more of what is spiritually possible for you as a child of God. Few Souls know or understand that God's Prophet can safely guide God's children, while still alive physically, to their Heavenly Home. Taking a child of God into the Heavens is not the job of clergy. Clergy have a responsibility to pass on the teaching of their religion exactly as they were taught, not to add additional concepts or possibilities. If every clergy member taught their own personal belief system no religion could survive for long. Then the beautiful teachings of an earlier Prophet of God would be lost. Clergy can be creative in finding interesting and uplifting ways to share their teachings, but their job is to keep their religion intact. However, God sends His Prophets to build on the teachings of His past Prophets, to share God's Light and Love, to teach His language, and to guide Souls to their Heavenly Home.

There is ALWAYS MORE when it comes to God's teachings and truth. No one Prophet can teach ALL of God's ways. It may be that the audience of a particular time in history cannot absorb more wisdom. It could be due to a

Prophet's limited time to teach and limited time in a physical body on Earth. Ultimately, it is that there is ALWAYS MORE! Each of God's Prophets brings additional teachings and opportunities for ways to draw closer to God, building on the work and teachings of former Prophets. That is one reason why Prophets of the past ask God to send another; to comfort, teach, and continue to help God's children grow into greater abundance. Former Prophets continue to have great love for God's children and want to see them continue to grow in accepting more of God's Love. One never needs to stop loving or accepting help from a past Prophet in order to grow with the help of the current Prophet. All true Prophets of God work together and help one another to do God's work.

All the testimonies in this book were written by students at the Guidance for a Better Life retreat center. It is here that the nature of God, the Holy Spirit, and the nature of Soul are EXPERIENCED under the guidance of a true living Prophet of God. Guidance for a Better Life is NOT a religion, it is a retreat center. God and His Prophet are NOT disparaging of any religion of love. However, the more a path defines itself with its teachings, dogma, or tenets, the more "walls" it inadvertently creates between the seeker and God. Sometimes it even puts God into a smaller box. God does not fit in any box. Prophet is for all Souls and is purposely not officially aligned with any path, but shows respect to all.

YOU can truly have an ABUNDANT LIFE through a personal and loving relationship with God, the Holy Spirit, and God's ordained Prophet. This is my primary message to you. Having a closer relationship with the Divine requires understanding the "Language of the Divine." God expresses His Love to us, His children, in many different and sometimes very subtle ways. Often His Love goes unrecognized and unaccepted because His language is not well known. The testimonies in this book have shown you some of the ways in which God expresses His Love. It is my hope that in reading this book, you have begun to learn more of the "Language of the Divine." The stories spanned from very subtle Divine guidance to profound examples of experiencing God up close and very personal. After reading this book I hope you now know your relationship with God has the potential to be more profound, more personal, and more loving than any organized religion on Earth currently teaches.

If you wish to develop a relationship with God's Prophet, seek the inner side of Prophet, for he is spiritually already with you. Few are able to meet the current physical incarnation and most people do not need to meet Prophet physically. Gently sing HU for a few minutes and then sing "Prophet" with love in your heart and he will respond. It may take time to recognize his presence, but it will come. The Light and Love that flows through him is the same that has flowed through all of God's true Prophets.

A more abundant life awaits you,

Prophet Del Hall III

Articles of Faith

Written by Prophet Del Hall III

1. There is one true God who is still living and active in our lives. He is knowable and wants a relationship with each of His children. He is the same God Jesus called FATHER and is known by many names, including Heavenly Father, and the ancient names for God, HU, and Sugmad (Pronounced SOOG-mahd). God wants a loving, trusting, personal relationship with each of us, NOT one based upon fear or guilt.

2. The Holy Spirit is God's expression in all the worlds. It is in two parts, the Light and the Sound. It is through His Holy Spirit God communicates and delivers all His gifts: peace, clarity, love, joy, healings, correction, guidance, wisdom, comfort, truth, dreams, new revelations, and more.

3. God always has a chosen living Prophet to teach His ways, speak His Living Word, lift up Souls, and bring us closer to God. God's living Prophet is a concentrated aspect of the Holy Spirit, the Light and Sound, and is raised up and ordained by God directly. His Prophet is

empowered and authorized to share God's Light and Sound and to correct misunderstandings of His ways. There are two aspects of God's Prophet, an inner spiritual and outer physical Prophet. The inner Prophet can teach us through dreams, intuition, spiritual travel, inner communication, and his presence. The outer Prophet also teaches through his discourses, written word, and his presence. There is no separation between the inner and outer Prophet. Both inner and outer aspects of Prophet are concentrated aspects of the Holy Spirit. Prophet is always with us spiritually on the inner. Prophet points to and glorifies the Father.

4. God so loves the world and His children He has always had a long unbroken line of His chosen Prophets on Earth. They existed before Jesus and after Jesus. Jesus was God's Prophet and His actual SON. God's chosen Prophets are considered to be in the "role of God's son," though NOT literally His Son. Only Jesus was literally His Son. Prophets were sometimes called Paraclete. The Bible uses the word Comforter, but the original Greek word was Paraclete, which is more accurate. Paraclete implies an actual physical person who helps, counsels,

encourages, advocates, comforts, sets free, and more.

5. Our real and eternal self is called Soul. We are Soul; we do NOT "have" a Soul. As Soul we are literally an individualized piece of God's Holy Spirit, thereby divine in nature. As an individual and uniquely experienced Soul you have free will, intelligence, imagination, opinions, clear and continuous access to Divine guidance, and immortality. As Soul we have an innate and profound spiritual growth potential. Soul has the ability to travel the Heavens spiritually with Prophet to gain truth and wisdom and grow in love. Soul exists because God loves It.

6. We have one eternal life as Soul. However, Soul needs to incarnate many times into a physical body to learn and grow spiritually mature. Soul's long journey back home to God where It was first created encompasses many lifetimes. A loving God does not expect His children to learn His ways in a single lifetime.

7. Soul equals Soul, in that God loves all Souls equally and each Soul has the same innate qualities and potential. Soul is neither male nor female, any particular race, nationality, or age. When Soul comes into a physical body at birth, the physical body is male or female, a certain

race, a nationality, and has an age. All Souls are children of God. We do not have to earn God's Love; He loves us unconditionally.

8. Soul incarnates on Earth to grow in the ability to give and receive love and learn to live the way God wishes us to live. Because God loves us, His ways of living create abundant, happy, fulfilling lives. His beautiful ways of living are mostly HOW to live, and less on what NOT to do.

9. God is more interested in two Souls learning to love one another regardless of their sexual preference. God loves you just the way you are.

10. It is God's will that a negative power exists to help Soul grow spiritually through challenges and hardships, thereby strengthening and maturing Soul. We are never given a challenge greater than our ability to find a solution to or understand the necessary lesson, if we use our God-given creativity, make sufficient personal effort, and ask for and accept the help available from the Divine. Soul has the ability to rise above any obstacles with God's help.

11. We study the Bible as an authentic teaching tool of God's ways, in addition to books and discourses authored by a Prophet chosen by God. We know the original biblical writings are

sometimes misunderstood, for example, God loves each of us regardless of our errors and shortcomings. God's eternal abandonment or damnation is not true. He would never turn His back to us for eternity. (Isaiah 54:7-8 and 10, Lamentations 3:31-32, and Hebrews 13:5)

12. Karma is the way in which the Divine accounts for our actions, words, thoughts, and attitudes. One can create positive or negative karma. Karma is a blessing used to teach us responsibility.

13. A child is not born in sin, however, the child does have karma from former lives. Karma, God's accounting system, explains our birth circumstances better than the concept of sin.

14. A living Prophet, including Jesus, can remove karma and sin when necessary to help us get started or to grow on the path home to God. However, it is primarily our responsibility to live and grow in the ways of God, thereby not creating negative karma and sin.

15. There are four commandments of God in which we abide: First — Love God with all your heart, mind, and Soul; Second — Love your neighbor as yourself. The Third is, "Seek ye first the Kingdom of God, and His righteousness."

This means that it is primarily our responsibility to draw close to God, learn His ways, and strive to live the way God would like us to live. God's Prophet is sent to show His ways. Our purpose, the Fourth Commandment, is to become spiritually mature to be used by God to bless His children. Becoming a coworker with God through His Comforter is our primary purpose in life and the most rewarding attainment of Soul.

16. All Souls upon translation, death of the physical body, go to the higher worlds, called Heavens, planes, or mansions, regardless of their beliefs. The way they live life on Earth and the effort made to draw close to God impacts the area of Heaven they are to be sent. Those who purposely harm others (except in defense of self or others), themselves, or live against the ways of God go to unpleasant locations on the first Heaven; to a location where they can learn how to do better, as a gift of love. The first Heaven has a wide range of locations, from very very unpleasant and hellish, to wonderful and beautiful places to spend time with loved ones while learning and preparing for future incarnations. Those who draw close to a Prophet of God, including Jesus, receive special care. We know of twelve distinct Heavens, not one. The

primary Abode of the Heavenly Father is in the twelfth Heaven, known as the Ocean of Love and Mercy. We can visit God while we still live on Earth, if taken by His chosen Prophet and only as Soul, not in a physical body.

17. Prayer is sacred, personal exchange with God and is an extreme privilege. God hears every prayer from the heart whether or not we recognize a response. Singing an ancient name of God, HU, is our foundational prayer. It expresses love and gratitude to God and is unencumbered by words. Singing HU has the potential to raise us up in consciousness making us more receptive to God's Love, Light, and guiding Hand. After praying it is best to spend time listening to God. Prayer should never be rote or routine. We desire to trust God and to know His will for us, and then freely and joyfully surrender to His will rather than our own will. God's Prophet can teach us the "Language of the Divine" which will help us understand how God communicates with us and help us recognize God's Love in our lives.

18. It is our responsibility to stay spiritually nourished. When Soul is nourished and fortified It becomes activated, and we are more receptive and have clearer communication with the Divine.

When Jesus said, "Give us this day our daily bread," he meant daily spiritual nourishment, not physical bread. The Holy Spirit is nourishment for Soul. This can be received by singing HU, studying Scripture, praying, dream study, demonstrating gratitude for our blessings, being in a living Prophet's physical presence or in his inner presence, or listening to his words.

19. TRUTH has the power to improve every area of our lives, but only if understood, accepted, and integrated into our lives.

20. God and His Prophet guide us in our sleeping dreams and awake dreams as a gift of love. God's Prophet teaches how to understand both types of dreams. All areas of our lives may be blessed by the wisdom God offers each of us directly in dreams.

21. Gratitude is extremely important on the path of love. It is literally the secret of love. Developing an attitude of gratitude is necessary to becoming spiritually mature. Recognizing and being grateful for the blessings of God in our lives is vital to building a loving and trusting relationship with God and His chosen Prophet. A relationship with God's Prophet is THE KEY to everything good. This includes a more abundant

life filled with the Treasures of Heaven Jesus taught about in Matthew 6.

22. We are to be good stewards of our blessings. We recognize them as gifts of love from God and make the effort to have remembrance. Remembering our blessings helps to keep our hearts open to God and builds trust in God's Love for us.

23. We give others the respect and freedom to have their own beliefs, make their own choices, and live their lives as they wish. We expect the same in return.

24. The Love and blessings of God and His Prophet are available to all who are receptive. If one desires guidance and help from Prophet, ask from the heart and sing "Prophet." He will respond. One does not need to meet Prophet physically to receive help because he is a concentrated aspect of God's Holy Spirit, and is always with us. To be taught by Prophet in the physical is a sacred blessing. Much can be gained by reading or listening to the Heavenly Father's teachings being shared by Prophet.

25. We have a responsibility to do our part and let God and His Prophet do their part. This responsibility brings freedom. Our goal is to

remain spiritually nourished, live the ways of God, live in balance with a core peace, and serve God as a coworker through His Comforter. We pray to use our God-given free will in a way that our actions, thoughts, words, and attitudes testify and bear witness to the Glory and Love of God.

26. There is always more to learn and grow in God's ways and truth. One cannot remain the same spiritually. One must make the effort to move forward or risk falling backward. To grow in consciousness and love requires change. Spiritual wisdom gained during our earthly incarnations can be taken to the other worlds when we translate, and into future lifetimes, unlike our physical possessions that remain in the physical.

Contact Information

Guidance for a Better Life is a worldwide mentoring program provided by Prophet Del Hall III and his son Del Hall IV. Personal one-on-one mentoring at our retreat center is our premier offering and the most direct and effective way to grow spiritually. Spiritual tools, guided exercises, and in-depth discourses on the eternal teachings of God are provided to help one become more aware of and receptive to His Holy Spirit and the abundance that awaits. With this personally-tailored guidance one begins to more fully recognize God's Love daily in their lives, both the dramatic and the very subtle. Over time our mentoring reduces fear, worry, anxiety, lack of purpose, feelings of unworthiness, guilt, and confusion; replacing those negative aspects of life with an abundance of peace, clarity, joy, wisdom, love, and self-respect leading to a more personal relationship with God, more than most know is possible. We also offer our videos, and more than twenty inspirational and educational books.

Guidance for a Better Life
P.O. Box 219
Lyndhurst, Virginia 22952
(540) 377-6068
contact@guidanceforabetterlife.com
www.guidanceforabetterlife.com

"A Growing Testament to the Power of God's Love One Profound Book at a Time."

If you could only read one of Prophet Del Hall's books this is the one. It is full of Keys to unlock the treasures of Heaven and bring more of God's Love into your life.

Spiritual Keys

For a More Abundant Life

PROPHET DEL HALL

Wayshowers are God's special emissaries to Earth. Our Heavenly Father loves us so much He has never left us alone without a Wayshower to teach us His true ways. This book explores the amazing history of God's chosen and ordained Wayshowers from thirty-five thousand years ago to today through specific examples of both well-known and little-known Wayshowers.

The
WAYSHOWER
TO
GOD

PROPHET DEL HALL

GOD IS IN THE GARDEN
PARABLES

Regardless of what your venture is in life you can benefit from this unassuming book. It may appear small, but the parables contained within have the power to affect your life in extraordinary ways.

GOD
IS IN THE
Garden

PARABLES
BY DEL HALL IV

ZOOM WITH PROPHET

Guidance for a Better Life retreat center has been hosting in-person mountaintop retreats at our beautiful location in the Blue Ridge Mountains of Virginia since 1990. When the pandemic began in 2020, it inspired us to get creative with how to connect with our students and new seekers. It was then our *Zoom With Prophet* meeting series was born. Some of these Zoom meetings are now being put into book form for those who could not attend.

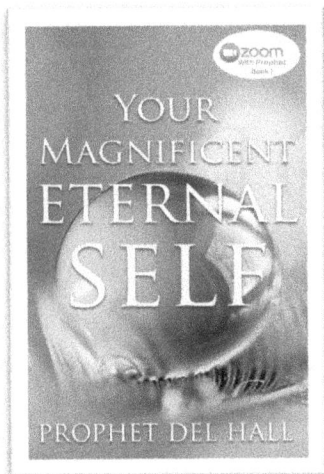

YOUR MAGNIFICENT ETERNAL SELF

PROPHET DEL HALL

BECOME Receptive to GOD'S LOVE

PROPHET DEL HALL

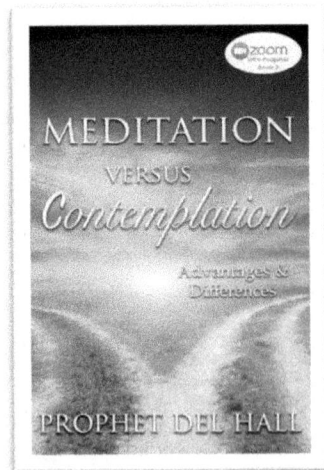

MEDITATION VERSUS Contemplation

Advantages & Differences

PROPHET DEL HALL

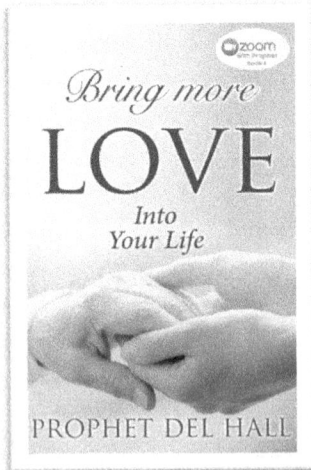

Bring more LOVE Into Your Life

PROPHET DEL HALL

SPECIALIZED TOPICS

Whether you wish to reconnect with a loved one who has passed, understand how you too can experience God's Light, improve your marriage, or learn how to understand your dreams, these incredible books have you covered.

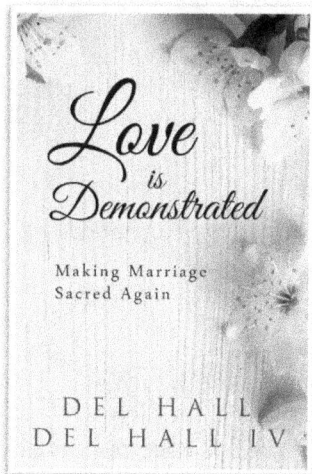

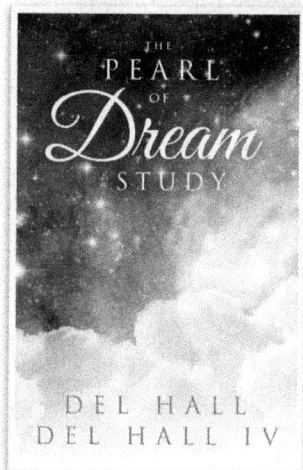

TESTIMONIES OF GOD'S LOVE SERIES

God expresses His Love every day in many different and sometimes subtle ways. Often this love goes unrecognized because the ways in which God communicates are not well known. Each of the books in this series contains fifty true stories that will help you learn to better recognize the Love of God in your life.

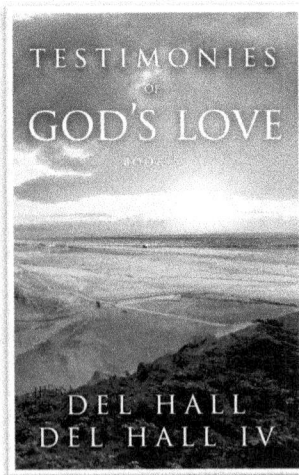

JOURNEY TO A TRUE SELF-IMAGE SERIES

This series includes intimate and unique stories that many readers will be able to personally identify with, enjoy, and learn from. They will help the reader transcend the false images people often carry about themselves — first and foremost that they are only their physical mind and body. The authors share their journeys of recognizing and coming to more fully accept their true self-image, that of Soul — an eternal child of God.

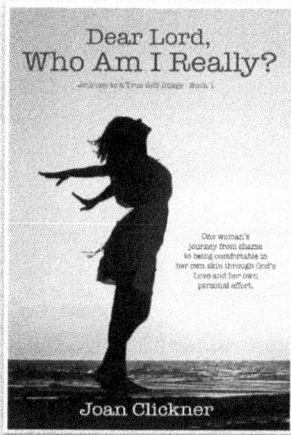

Dear Lord, Who Am I Really?
Journey to a True Self-Image - Book 1
One woman's journey from shame to being comfortable in her own skin through God's Love and her own personal effort.
Joan Clickner

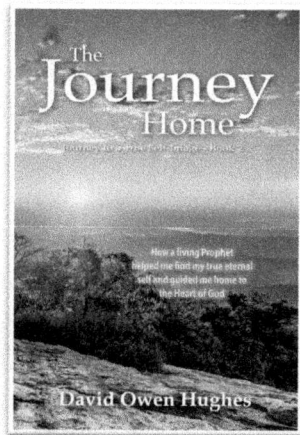

The Journey Home
Journey to a True Self-Image - Book 2
How a living Prophet helped me find my true eternal self and guided me home to the Heart of God
David Owen Hughes

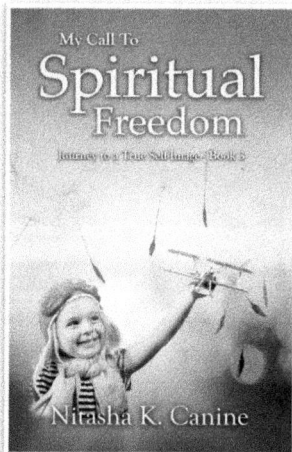

My Call To Spiritual Freedom
Journey to a True Self-Image - Book 3
Nitasha K. Canine

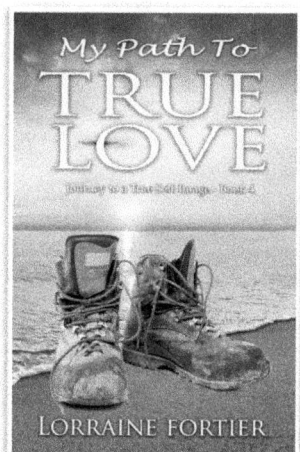

My Path To TRUE LOVE
Journey to a True Self-Image - Book 4
LORRAINE FORTIER

www.ingramcontent.com/pod-product-compliance
Lightning Source LLC
Chambersburg PA
CBHW060230050426
42448CB00009B/1369